The Twisted Chain

KA HAEA TE ATA

The Twisted Chain

A conversation about levelling the playing field

Jason Gurney

OTAGO UNIVERSITY PRESS
Te Whare Tā o Ōtākou Whakaihu Waka

For Keg

Contents

Prologue	7
Introduction	9
Chapter One **Infection**	13
Chapter Two **Response**	27
Chapter Three **Rheumatic fever: Discovery, failure, repeat**	33
Chapter Four **Gone, not gone**	45
Chapter Five **The long shadow**	55
Chapter Six **The causes of rheumatic fever**	75
Chapter Seven **The causes of the causes I: Poor housing**	91
Chapter Eight **The causes of the causes II: Poverty and power**	109
Chapter Nine **The path forward**	129
Epilogue	137
Acknowledgements	145
Notes	147

Prologue

WINTER, 1969. On a paddock in the rural outskirts of Auckland, a regional schoolboy rugby tournament is taking place. One of the competing teams has made the almost 200-kilometre trip from Whangārei in an old Bedford bus. The boys have set up makeshift sleeping quarters in the gymnasium of a local high school. For the next three days, they will share crowded barracks. It will rain incessantly, and it won't be long before everyone is damp, cold and tired. On the way back to Whangārei after the tournament, people will be coughing and sneezing. For at least one player on the bus, the illness everyone seems to have caught will turn out to be much more serious than an attack of the sniffles.

That player was a nippy 14-year-old halfback known as Keg – a nickname given to him when he was a chubby child. Keg returned to his mum and dad with what seemed a nasty cold. As the days passed, Keg's condition deteriorated. His throat was acutely inflamed, and when he swallowed his saliva felt like shards of glass. He developed a fever so intense he thought he would catch fire. His ankles and wrists ached with a lasting ferocity, well beyond what was typical after a hard-fought footy tournament.

Lethargic and in pain, Keg spent the next two months in bed and the following four months convalescing. The tedium was broken by visits to Whangārei Hospital for further tests. Although his joints hurt a lot, for some reason his doctors were most interested in his heart. He was constantly being asked to bare his chest for a stethoscope's touch: *Breathe in, breathe out; in, and out again.*

The doctors had good reason to be concerned. Keg had been diagnosed with rheumatic fever. A bacterial infection had lit the fuse, but a quirk in his immune defence system had caused a damaging response, and his body had suffered a massive attack on many fronts. The devastating consequences of this response would be with him for the rest of his life.

∽

Summer, 1982. Keg is waiting in the same hospital he has visited many times since that tournament in 1969. His legs bounce with impatience. He's waiting to see his newborn son. The baby has jaundice and is being cared for in the intensive care unit under ultraviolet light. When visiting time finally arrives, Keg cradles the child and rocks him back and forth in his arms, murmuring in a low voice to soothe his cries.

I was that jaundiced boy, and Keg is my dad. This book is for him.

Introduction

I GREW UP KNOWING that something was wrong with my father's heart. It didn't seem too serious to me – he was (and still is) full of joy for life and appeared to have abundant energy. But in my teenage years, things started to go haywire for Dad. Every other month he would be rushed to hospital. Sometimes we wouldn't call an ambulance because Dad didn't think we could wait that long. On those occasions, I'd drive him helter-skelter to the emergency room at Auckland's Middlemore Hospital. Once there I'd sit at his bedside while he closed his eyes and waited for help. He'd tell me that everything was going to be okay, and I'd try to reassure him too. Nevertheless, every 10 minutes or so, I'd excuse myself for a panicked sob next to the water cooler.

The cause of these urgent trips to the hospital was a chronic health condition called rheumatic heart disease. It's the most serious long-term consequence of rheumatic fever, an autoimmune illness precipitated by a bacterial infection. Rheumatic fever typically occurs during childhood, affecting children around the same age Dad was when he suffered the illness. It commonly begins with a sore throat but can also start from a skin infection. The condition can cause the heart to swell and delicate heart tissue to be attacked and damaged by our own immune system. Almost all the morbidity and mortality caused by rheumatic fever is due to rheumatic heart disease. Not everyone who gets rheumatic fever will go on to develop rheumatic heart disease, but for those who do, the condition is both life-altering and life-shortening.

Not knowing if your dad will live through the night is not something that any young son or daughter should ever have to endure. I experienced this nightmare more times than I care to remember. Looking back, I can easily see how those experiences shaped me and influenced my decision to embark on a career in public health. Getting involved in rheumatic fever research was my way of fighting back against the illness that had changed the trajectory of my family's life.

Eventually, my work on rheumatic fever saw me take on the role of manager of the largest national study undertaken so far on the causes of this illness. Yet, despite my intense relationship with rheumatic fever over so many years – both as my father's son and as a scientist – I realised I still had large gaps in my understanding of this disease. Where had it come from? How did it happen? And why did it choose my dad but miss other schoolboys at that tournament in 1969? To fill these gaps, I began to do more research of my own, going right back to first principles, to build a more complete picture of the illness. That research was the genesis of this book.

The Twisted Chain of the title refers to several important factors that influence the rheumatic fever story. Firstly, the bacteria that cause the infection that can lead to rheumatic fever are a type of *Streptococcus* that have the characteristic *Streptococcus* shape of a twisted chain when viewed under the microscope. But rheumatic fever is not caused by the *Streptococcus* infection per se. Rather, it is caused by the immune system's response to the infection, which consists of a chain of events intended to defeat the bacterial infection.

The immune system response contains an inherent twist, whereby in its eagerness to defeat the invading bacteria, it may also attack and damage some of the body's own cells. This is the second 'twisted chain' of the book's title. The third is a social one, the demographic warp that continues to hold some populations within the tight grasp of the disease, despite the near-eradication of rheumatic fever from most developed countries. The statistics for Aotearoa New Zealand reveal this twist starkly. Rates of rheumatic fever and rheumatic heart disease experienced by some groups in New Zealand are among the highest in the world, comparable to those experienced in developing countries. Māori and Pacific peoples are disproportionately affected, collectively making up more than 90 percent of diagnosed cases. A Māori child growing up in New Zealand is around 17 times more likely to develop rheumatic fever than a child of European ethnicity. A Pacific child is nearly 30 times as likely to get this disease.

The first half of this book, from Chapter One to Chapter Five, explores the first two of these twisted chains: infection by *Streptococcus*, and the immune response. The second half, from Chapter Six to Chapter Nine, focuses more on the third twisted chain, especially the effects of social inequity on rates of rheumatic fever. Throughout, you will find Keg's story, because whenever anyone gets rheumatic fever, their life is forever changed, as are the lives of all who love them.

Chapter One
Infection

WHEN I WAS EIGHT OR NINE I learned that my grandfather – Keg's dad – had been a soldier in World War II. He rarely spoke about his experience, but his 17 grandchildren were naïve enough to ask questions that his five children had not, and we got more out of him than they had. Still, it wasn't much. So I turned to history books to quench my thirst for war-related knowledge. I read all 10 volumes of a World War I encyclopaedia stored in our attic and hoarded thick biographies of famous soldiers and military leaders to read in bed at night. I became especially interested in why wars began. Reading about the fear of communism spreading in Vietnam or the rise of Nazism out of Weimar Germany, I came to learn that world-changing events don't come out of nowhere: many things need to coalesce to initiate them.

With rheumatic fever, one of the initiating factors is infection. What causes infection, and why do some people have very mild symptoms while others get very sick? Even in the twenty-first century, these questions are not fully answerable. Two centuries ago, without knowledge of bacteria and viruses and without an understanding of how the immune system reacts to infection, answers were impossible. I realised early in my research for this book that we can't understand rheumatic fever without understanding both sides of the equation: invasion by bacteria *and* response by the immune system. This chapter focuses on the invasion, and Chapter 2 will focus on the immune response.

∽

Reading about the complex causes of World War I (1914–1918) led me to the decades-earlier Franco-Prussian War (1870–1871), which had its roots in the unwelcome (for the French) prospect of the unification of most German-speaking European states. Keen to extinguish the spark of that prospect before it could catch fire, the French, under Napoleon III, went to war. When the Franco-Prussian War ended less than a year later, more than 180,000 soldiers were dead, and more than 200,000 were wounded. It was through reading about that war and those terrible losses – particularly in the battle of Weissenburg in August 1870 – that I first came across a man called Theodor Billroth.

Billroth was not a soldier; he was a professor of surgery at the University of Vienna. In 1859 he published a comprehensive overview of the history of gunshot wound treatment from the fifteenth to the nineteenth centuries.[1] When the Franco-Prussian War broke out, he saw a chance to make his mark in medical history and volunteered for service immediately. He arrived in Weissenburg on the day of a major, devastating battle and before long had Weissenburg's medical staff and facilities marching to his drum.

Billroth was unusual for his time in recognising the harm caused by wound infection. He was a proponent of the then-controversial ideas of antiseptic surgery and post-operative care. He practised improved techniques of hygienic amputation and ordered that fastidious attention be paid to any sign of post-surgical infection. The results for his patients were excellent, and his report detailing the lessons learned became a foundational text in military medicine.[2]

After the Franco-Prussian War ended in 1871, Billroth's obsession with wound infection grew. He returned to Vienna and experimented with specimens of infected tissue, applying broths of his own concoctions and recording the effects of each. He was fascinated with the culture and growth of the bacteria that he saw under the microscope. In 1874, he published his observations in a book, *Coccobacteria Septica*.[3]

This book was more of a diary than a textbook.[4] In it, Billroth described and drew the microorganisms he had studied during his experiments with infected tissue. One bacterium in particular stood out, its physical shape resembling the twists of a chain. Taking the Greek words for necklace (*streptos*) and berry (*coccus*), he named it *Streptococcus* – 'necklace of berries' – and recorded this next to his drawing of the curious discovery.

In the twenty-first century it is common knowledge that infections in the human body are caused by microorganisms, usually fungi, viruses or bacteria. Billroth, however, could not have understood the significance of his finding at the time. In identifying *Streptococcus*, he had discovered a family of bacteria more damaging to humans than all the bullets and shells fired at people during the deadly Franco-Prussian War.

∞

Bacteria are tiny organisms with perhaps the most unfair reputation of all living things. Yes, bacteria can cause stomach cramps, irritating skin sores and wheezy lungs, but the reality is that more than 99 percent of all known bacteria are good for us, helping us digest food or fight off harmful organisms.[5] Even bacteria with scary-sounding names, such as *Escherichia coli* (or *E. coli*), usually live happily inside our lower intestines, where they help break down food and extract the nutrients we need to live. *E. coli* bacteria only cause vicious cramps if we eat contaminated food and the bacteria land up in the stomach, a part of our digestive system where they are not supposed to be.

Bacteria are so small they cannot be seen by the human eye without magnification. Despite this, they are complex organisms. For example, they have the ability to make copies of themselves. Viruses, although smaller and less intricate than bacteria, also possess the ability to replicate themselves. Both bacteria and viruses thrive by finding a host environment in which to live. A human body is often the ideal host. A crucial difference between bacteria and viruses is how they treat the cells in their host environment. Viruses do not have an independent metabolism and must, therefore, plunder the metabolism of their host's cells in order to survive and replicate. This means that a viral infection frequently results in the death of the cells infected by the virus.[6] Bacteria, being more complex organisms, do have their own metabolic processes. They can cause damage to their host cells without necessarily killing them.

The human body's response to the invasion of undesirable microorganisms, such as viruses and bacteria, is managed by the immune system. The goal of the immune response is to make the body as inhospitable as possible for the microorganism. This is why we vomit or spike a fever. These unpleasant symptoms of illness are not directly caused by the invading viruses or bacteria. Instead, they are part of the way our immune system tries to eliminate these invaders and ensure our survival.

Our immune system is complex and effective, yet it can also be blunt and imprecise – even, we could say, a bit twisted. Rheumatic fever is an excellent example of just such a twisted immune response.

∽

In the century and a half following Billroth's discovery of *Streptococcus,* it has become clear that this strain of bacteria consists of many unique species. Some of these breathe life into common food products. Streptococci species are used to make yoghurt since they help turn the sugar in milk (lactose) into lactic acid. Importantly, from my pizza-loving perspective, streptococci add acidity and flavour to soft cheeses such as mozzarella.[7]

In fact, nearly all species of *Streptococcus* are either good for us or completely harmless. However, there are exceptions. *Streptococcus agalactia* is the culprit behind many cases of meningitis in newborn babies.[8] *Streptococcus pneumoniae* causes a significant proportion of all cases of both meningitis and pneumonia.[9] But the species that Keg encountered at his rugby tournament might just be the blackest of this family's sheep. Its scientific name is *Streptococcus pyogenes*, but it is often referred to as *Group-A Strep*.

Group-A Strep is made up of spherical cells that cling together to form the twisted chains observed by Billroth in the 1870s. Each cell in the chain measures about one micron in diameter – or one one-thousandth of a millimetre – and is coated by a capsule covered in fine, hair-like fibres, which are superb at sticking to the walls of human cells.[10] Once the *Group-A Strep* cells are attached to, say, the walls of the throat, they hunker down and do their best to avoid or destroy the body's immune system defences.

We now know that *Group-A Strep* is the most adaptable strain of the entire *Streptococcus* family if not one of the most adaptable pathogens in existence.[11] For example, the capsule that surrounds a *Group-A Strep* cell is made of an acid that not only helps it stick to the host's cell walls, but also to tunnel into the interior of the host cell. This trick is difficult for the immune system to figure out in time to prevent the body's cells from being invaded.

To make things even more difficult for our immune system, there is not only one kind of *Group-A Strep*. At least 200 nuanced sub-types have been identified.[12] This has profound implications for how well our body develops immunity following a *Group-A Strep* infection because immunity is only established for the particular sub-type that caused the infection.

It is not unusual for people to be hosting *Group-A Strep* in their bodies without knowing it. This 'silent carriage' is remarkably common, especially in children. Around 12 percent of all children carry this type of bacteria in their throats without developing a symptomatic infection.[13] Because they are blissfully unaware that they are carrying infectious bacteria, this cohort of people make perfect transport vehicles for *Group-A Strep*, which will take every opportunity to jump from the carrier to a new host. The problem is that the new host may not be as immunologically fit as the carrier.

∞

Billroth's identification of *Streptococcus* in the 1870s came at a time when the study of bacteria was gathering momentum, and a new concept of disease transmission known as germ theory was beginning to emerge. Germ theory, made famous by such researchers as French microbiologist Louis Pasteur and German physician Robert Koch, said that infectious diseases were caused by small organisms called germs.[14] Before germ theory, it was widely believed that these diseases were caused by a poisonous mist called 'miasma', or 'bad air', which wafted from decomposing corpses and other rotting organic matter. Miasma theory got some things right: rotting corpses *are* fabulous breeding grounds for microorganisms, and pathogens such as the SARS-CoV-2 virus that causes COVID-19 *can* spread through the air.[15] But the scientists of Billroth's era had begun to understand that the miasma theory was insufficient as an explanation of disease transmission. For example, in blaming the spread of disease on vapour arising from dead tissue, the miasma theory did not allow for the possibility that illness could be carried and spread by living people.

Billroth's discovery of *Streptococcus* enabled great strides toward understanding the link between these particular bacteria and human disease. Louis Pasteur, for example, studied puerperal fever, or 'childbed fever' as it was known. Puerperal fever is an infection of the female reproductive organs following childbirth. It can lead to sepsis and death and was a common cause of maternal mortality in Pasteur's time. In 1879, he took a sample of a dying mother's blood and viewed it through his microscope. He recognised the twisted chains described by Billroth: streptococcal bacteria, not miasma, was the cause of puerperal fever.[16]

Pasteur's discovery explained what Hungarian obstetrician Ignaz Semmelweis had observed in the 1840s in his work at Vienna General Hospital. Semmelweis had focused on puerperal fever and the horrific mortality rates it caused. He noticed the relatively high number of mothers who died shortly after giving birth on his ward, a ward run by doctors. In contrast, post-partum deaths were substantially lower in the adjacent ward, which was led by nurses. Looking back at the hospital records, Semmelweis saw that throughout the 1840s the total post-birth death rate was 10 percent in the doctor-led ward but only three percent in the nurse-led ward.[17]

Like a detective puzzling out a clue, Semmelweis considered the possible causes of the difference in death rates between the two wards. Perhaps the mothers who were admitted to the doctor-led ward were sicker when they arrived than the mothers who were admitted to the nurse-led ward. The sicker the mother was when she was admitted, his reasoning went, the greater the chance she would die. But Semmelweis had to discount this possibility when his research revealed that none of the mothers who had died of puerperal fever had already been sick when they arrived on the maternity ward.

Semmelweis eventually traced the anomaly in survival outcomes to a difference in how the two wards were run. Vienna General was a teaching hospital, and junior doctors were routinely ushered into the morgue to examine the bodies of women who had died on the ward, including those who had died of puerperal fever. Afterwards, the doctors (including Semmelweis himself) continued their normal rounds. These rounds included examinations of healthy women, many of whom had yet to deliver their babies. The doctors were transferring streptococcal bacteria on their hands from the morgue to the wards and, in doing so, they were killing their patients.

Although he did not know exactly what was contaminating the doctors' hands, Semmelweis introduced chlorine hand washes for his staff. The washes were introduced in May 1847, at which time the death rate was 12 percent. By July 1847, after just two months of this small change in clinical routine, the death rate on the wards had plummeted to one percent. It seemed beyond doubt that chlorine was effective in saving the lives of new mothers but, unfortunately, scientists in the 1840s remained in thrall to miasma theory. While history would go on to recognise him as a medical revolutionary, in his time Semmelweis was widely panned and discredited for his strange theories about the transmission of infectious diseases. Without knowledge of the existence of bacteria he could not adequately explain how the doctors were introducing infection to the hospital ward. At the age of just 47, he suffered a nervous breakdown and was committed to a mental asylum.[18] After only two weeks there, Semmelweis died of septicaemia caused by a wound that had developed a bacterial infection.

∽

While it came far too late for Semmelweis, Pasteur's finding in 1879 that puerperal fever was spread by bacteria occurred during a new age of discovery about *Streptococcus*. In 1873, German surgeon Friedrich Fehleisen had discovered the bacteria were associated with the development of erysipelas (a bright red skin infection). In 1874, German physician and microbiologist Friedrich Rosenbach identified a similar strain of *Streptococcus* in a patient's wound. He named it *Streptococcus pyogenes* after the pus it produced during infection. As noted above, this strain is now known as *Group-A Strep*.[19]

In 1885, Edmund Klein, an anatomy lecturer from St Bartholomew's Hospital in London, was sent to investigate a community outbreak of scarlet fever, a highly contagious and (at the time) often fatal disease whose symptoms include a scalding fever, a strawberry-hued tongue and a scarlet body rash.[20] (Eventually it became evident that scarlet fever is a relatively superficial disease, with its rash and red tongue serving as indicators of an escalating *Group-A Strep* infection.[21] Death rarely comes from the fever itself, but rather from the uncontrolled progression from scarlet fever to the more dangerous consequences of *Group-A Strep* infection, discussed later in this chapter.)

Klein's mission was to attempt to establish the source of the scarlet fever outbreak so that a quarantine could be established. Before antibiotics, only public health measures such as quarantine were available to fight the disease. Klein went from patient to patient, eventually arriving on the outskirts of London at a farm that supplied milk to the city.[22] At the farm, he found that the cows were suffering from a skin disease, with severe ulcers on their udders and teats. Klein took a specimen. Later, in his London laboratory, he inspected it under his microscope. He saw a species of bacteria with a remarkable resemblance to that defined by Rosenbach in 1874 as *Streptococcus pyogenes*. Here again was *Group-A Strep*.

Klein had found a potential source of the scarlet fever outbreak – milk contaminated with bacteria from ulcerated udders – but to make a convincing link he now needed to compare the bacteria from the udders with bacteria found in people suffering from scarlet fever.

He recruited the help of a doctor at a local hospital that specialised in this disease. Klein's colleague took him to several patients ravaged by acute scarlet fever, and Klein drew blood from them. He put the samples under a microscope and found the same species of bacteria as on the ulcerated udders: *Group-A Strep*.

Klein reported his findings to the Royal Society, where he declared the source of London's scarlet fever epidemic to be a bacterial infection spread by contaminated milk. Yet, until hygienic food handling practices and pasteurisation (named after Louis Pasteur) became the norm in the late nineteenth and early twentieth century, infected milk would continue to cause many more outbreaks of *Group-A Strep* infection.[23]

∞

Throughout the twentieth century, the list of diseases found to be caused by *Group-A Strep* grew. These diseases ranged widely in severity, from relatively superficial illnesses such as scarlet fever to rarer and more serious secondary conditions. The broken-glass swallow that accompanies some sore throats was linked to *Group-A Strep* infection, giving rise to the term 'strep throat'. Additionally, it was discovered that *Group-A Strep* can cause infections like impetigo (also known as 'school sores') when it enters the body through broken skin.[24] These skin infections have an array of unpleasant symptoms, ranging from maddening itchiness to a rash so severe that the sufferer, usually a child, feels as if their skin is on fire.

Perhaps the most frightening of all skin diseases is a condition that brings to mind a B-grade horror film. Writing in *The American Surgeon* in the early 1950s, Robert Wilson described a disease that progressed rapidly, caused extreme pain and invaded the layers of tissue beneath the skin.[25] Wilson identified *Group-A Strep* as one of the main culprits behind this infection. He noted the bacteria's rapid growth along the fascia – the sheaths separating our muscles – which caused the surrounding tissues to break down and die in a process called necrosis.[26] Wilson labelled the disease 'necrotising fasciitis', but it is often simply called 'flesh-eating disease'. The infection can be so severe that the diseased tissue 'melts' away.[27] The patient then faces surgery: skin grafts or even amputation if the limb is beyond salvage.

Another rare but catastrophic result of infection by *Group-A Strep* is streptococcal toxic shock syndrome. This rare syndrome caused the death from multiple organ failure of *The Muppets* creator Jim Henson in 1990. An untreated *Group-A Strep* infection spread from Henson's throat to his respiratory system and organs, leading to widespread tissue damage, organ failure and death.

Diseases such as scarlet fever, necrotising fasciitis and streptococcal toxic shock syndrome are the direct consequence of *Group-A Strep* infection, where the bacteria wreak damage on the host's cells by releasing a barrage of toxins. For example, one such toxin punches through the walls of blood vessels close to the surface of the skin, producing the red rash that gives scarlet fever its name.[28] Jim Henson's death was largely the result of the sheer load of toxins that were circulating around his body, which caused whole organ systems to simply shut down.

Usually, though, the most serious effects of *Group-A Strep* infection, including rheumatic fever, do not manifest until after the *Streptococcus* bacteria have left the body. The disease known as *post-Streptococcal glomerulonephritis* – a linguistic mouthful, as well as a severe, life-threatening inflammation of the parts of the kidney that filter our blood – doesn't strike until weeks after *Group-A Strep* infection. It was this disease that cut short the incandescent career of musician and composer Wolfgang Amadeus Mozart at the age of just 35.[29] Two days after his final performance, Mozart fell ill and retired to his bedroom in Vienna, never to emerge again.

The condition that killed Mozart was a consequence of the same perverse twist in our body's natural response that, in 1969 in West Auckland, sent Keg's immune system into free fall. And it's this twist that lies at the heart of our story.

∞

Winter, 1969. Keg is 14 and has just arrived at his rugby home ground in Whangārei. He shoulders his rucksack, says goodbye to his mum and joins his teammates in the car park. Joking and laughing, they wait for the Bedford bus to arrive. When it comes, the boys climb aboard, jostling for seats and settling down to share the unventilated space for a three-hour journey.

While it's impossible to say for sure, it's entirely feasible that one or more of Keg's teammates was a carrier of *Group-A Strep*. The close quarters these teens shared over the next three days, starting with this bus trip, provided the perfect opportunity for the highly contagious bacteria to pass from person to person.

Let's assume that one of Keg's teammates – I'll call him Billy – is carrying *Group-A Strep* in his throat. As they board the bus, Billy might have no symptoms at all. Maybe he has a sore throat and a bit of a cough. In Auckland, the bus pulls in at a local high school, where the team is billeted for three days. Here, in the gymnasium, 20 boys share everything from water bottles to bedding. The building is unheated. Their clothes and gear are damp from the rainy weather and do not dry out all weekend.

After a miserable afternoon of wet footy, the team retreats to the gym. Billy throws his pillow down next to Keg's, and the two try to fall asleep. The gym is cold, the sleeping bags clammy. Next to Keg, Billy begins to cough in earnest.

By morning, the coughing has spread from boy to boy. They are sleep-deprived zombies. Few are fit for another day of tackling and running, but nonetheless they get ready. Exhausted, Keg slips on his muddy boots and laces up.

∽

Keg does not know it, but some of the several million *Group-A Strep* cells living in the back of Billy's throat have passed to him. During the night, with Keg and Billy lying close, one of Billy's coughs has propelled them in Keg's direction.

Chapter Two
Response

WE ARE BORN with an immature immune system that, throughout childhood, develops into a complex and adaptable defence network, involving most of the human body. For instance, our skin is more than just a stretchy outer layer; it is also a barrier against infection, our tightly packed skin cells providing a strong protective layer around us.[1] Other cells and organs intimately involved in providing the body's immune support include the thymus, spleen, bone marrow and lymph nodes.

Maybe because of my misspent youth reading so much military history, I find it useful to understand the immune system using metaphors of battle: attack and defence; opposing armies; camouflage, ambush and subterfuge; loss and victory; casualties and survivors. Our white blood cells, or leukocytes, for example, are stealth warriors, analogous to paramilitary troops. They deploy a strategy called phagocytosis, a process whereby they completely surround invading bacteria and rip them to shreds.[2] Leukocytes are also excellent communicators. As soon as they arrive at the scene of a bacterial infection, they send a message to nearby blood vessels, instructing them to douse the infection site in water. Flooding the area with fluid makes it easier for leukocytes to destroy bacteria. This early part of the immune response is why we notice swelling around the area of an infection.

If this proves insufficient to win the battle, the leukocytes call for reinforcements in the form of another type of white blood cell phagocyte called neutrophils, which flow through the bloodstream to the battleground.[3] Neutrophils unleash potent toxins that kill the invading bacteria – and, unfortunately, any of the body's own healthy cells that happen to be in the firing line. They are such effective cellular killing machines that, in order to minimise the damage they cause to their host, they are programmed to self-destruct after about five days.

This combined white blood cell response is enough to contain and destroy most bacterial invasions. However, if phagocytosis doesn't work, our immune system changes its strategy and sends for antibodies. Antibodies are tiny Y-shaped proteins that circulate in the bloodstream. When called to an infection site, they quickly surround and attach themselves to the invading bacteria.[4] They act like locator beacons, pinpointing the site of the battle so that another round of phagocyte reinforcements can be sent in. In this way, antibodies boost the immune system's response, helping our white blood cells track down their target with precision.

After our immune system has successfully fought off infection and killed the bacteria, most of the immune cells destroy themselves.[5] They do this so that they don't use up nutrients that could be better used in the healing process that will follow. However, the immune system always preserves a few veterans of the conflict. These are B and T cells, also known as memory cells because of their ability to recognise a familiar enemy in the future.[6] If we encounter the same bacterial invader again – say, a certain strain of *Group-A Strep* – the B and T cells ensure they are targeted and destroyed. Memory cells are the reason vaccination works.

Generally, when the immune system is in fighting form, it attacks and destroys the invader. Sometimes, however, the immune system is a victim of its own subterfuge. As we will soon learn, rheumatic fever is a perfect example of this.

∽

A *Group-A Strep* cell can't live for long outside a human host. It needs moist organic tissue to cling to in order to keep living.[7] In humans, *Group-A Strep* can survive in only two places: the throat (specifically the pharynx, at the back of our throats) or the skin. If it's on the skin, the *Group-A Strep* will enter our bodies only if the skin is broken.[8] But the pharynx is a major thoroughfare for all the essentials of life – water, food and oxygen – and so it is always open for docking.

Even a moist pharynx is an alien environment for *Group-A Strep*. In order to survive, the bacteria must pillage any useful nutrients they can find, and try to multiply as quickly as possible. Often, they remain undetected by the human body while they are doing this. Indeed, staying under cover for as long as possible is so helpful to *Group-A Strep* that this strain of bacteria has evolved to exploit this strategy. Like a warship that hides its flag until the other side is within cannon shot, *Group-A Strep* tries to fool its host into thinking it isn't a foreign invader at all. It's a clever molecular subterfuge that buys time and allows the bacteria to get firmly established in stolen territory.

Eventually, though, the human immune system recognises the presence of *Group-A Strep* and launches an attack. Ideally, things happen as described above: white blood cells pour in from the surrounding bloodstream and the immune system successfully chases down the invading cells, enveloping them and ripping them to shreds. However, because *Group-A Strep* has been evolving alongside the human immune system for millennia, it has more tricks to play. The battle scene intensifies.

The bacteria make a protein that attaches to the immune system's white blood cells. This protein switches off receptors on the white blood cells, stopping them from attaching themselves to the bacteria, and so preventing the immune system from destroying the bacterial cells.[9] When the white blood cells sense this happening, they fight back, releasing their own cascade of proteins and DNA around the infection site, weaving a net in which to catch the bacteria. In response, *Group-A Strep* drops a protein that specifically attacks the net's strands of DNA and another that punches holes in the walls of the white blood cells, destroying them.[10]

A successful *Group-A Strep* invasion occurs when the bacteria win enough of this battle against our immune system to establish a base of operations, covering the surface of the pharynx and penetrating the surrounding cells. This is a key and necessary step in the pathway toward rheumatic fever.

∽

On the second day of the tournament, as wet and miserable Keg ties his mud-encrusted bootlaces, the opening salvos in a microscopic war are being fired at the back of his throat. After passing from Billy to Keg the night before, *Group-A Strep* cells are latching onto the cells that line his pharynx and beginning to pry open gaps in the cell walls. The enemy storms in. Soon, Keg's throat is covered in bacteria, which are copying themselves and rapidly proliferating.

After the long bus trip back to Whangārei, he complains to his mother of a tickly throat. A day or so later, the tickle becomes a sharp stab. Peering into his mouth, his mother sees long white trails covering his tonsils and a raw-looking scarlet patch at the back of his throat. They visit a doctor, who says it is a textbook case of streptococcal pharyngitis: strep throat. He prescribes a course of penicillin and tells Keg's mother to bring him back if his symptoms worsen.

One week after stepping on the Bedford bus, and despite his mother's and doctor's best efforts, Keg is in trouble. The back of his throat is the scene of a microscopic war, and his immune system is in pitched battle with *Group-A Strep*, producing antibodies and phagocytes to shred the bacteria. Because Keg grew up in a lower-middle-class and crowded home in the far north of New Zealand, this is probably not his first encounter with *Group-A Strep*. His immune system has seen this foe before, and, for the most part, his memory cells are responding as expected.

At some point, however, the system meant to defend Keg begins overcompensating. His immune system receives a message to make antibodies that not only bind to *Group-A Strep* but to any cells that resemble *Group-A Strep* as well. This is a major problem, rather like police responding to a bank robbery, looking at security footage, and then ordering officers to look for a middle-aged man wearing a white t-shirt. It's only a matter of time before the wrong person gets fingered for the crime.

These antibodies flood Keg's body. They find the *Group-A Strep* cells, and phagocytes attack. However, antibodies also identify innocent cells, including the healthy cellular building blocks for the tissues of Keg's knees, ankles, elbows and wrists – and his heart. Now, cells that are nowhere near Keg's throat and have nothing at all to do with his current sickness are under friendly fire.

Rather than improving in response to the penicillin, Keg's condition worsens. Just two weeks after the rugby tournament, he cannot get out of bed. He has no energy, and his knees and ankles are constantly throbbing. He struggles to catch his breath.

The doctor is called again, and this time he makes a house visit. As he examines Keg, his face reveals deep concern. He tells Keg's mother that her son has something much more serious than strep throat. He has rheumatic fever and needs a cardiologist immediately.

She is puzzled. How can Keg's sore throat have anything to do with his heart? She begins to arrange transport to the hospital, but the doctor tells her not to. Keg should not leave his bed because the pressure exerted on his heart from standing could be dangerous. The cardiologist will come to him.

Later that day, the cardiologist arrives and places his stethoscope on Keg's chest. He says nothing until his examination is finished. He then turns to Keg's mother with a solemn expression and asks her to see him out. As they walk to the door, the cardiologist tells her that her son is very sick and that his heart has been damaged. He will need more tests, but first, and most importantly, he needs to rest.

Keg remains in bed for two months. He is housebound for another four, only leaving home for medical tests at Whangārei Hospital. Eventually, he begins to regain his energy, and his joint pains fade away. By the following rugby season, he has recovered enough to train with his old team again. Things begin to return to normal.

But rheumatic fever casts a long shadow. The results of Keg's immune system's strategic failings will eventually catch up with him.

Chapter Three
Rheumatic fever: Discovery, failure, repeat

KEG'S IMMUNE RESPONSE to the *Group-A Strep* infection was normal. Millennia of evolution have resulted in an immune system able to fight off bacteria that would have brought his ancestors low. Yet this same immune system response ultimately turned those early victories into defeat, a cruel twist that left him fighting for his life against a condition that neither he nor his family fully understood.

So, what is rheumatic fever?

Rheumatic fever is one of a family of diseases known as autoimmune disorders, where our own immune system becomes both villain and victim. It isn't something you 'catch' like a cold. Rather, it occurs when the body is invaded by *Group-A Strep* microorganisms, which then trigger a dangerously excessive immune response. This multi-system response leads to a cascade of inflammation around the body, most seriously in the delicate heart tissue. There is almost always a delay of days or even weeks between the initial infection with *Group-A Strep* and the immune system's overreaction, which means that diagnosing this disease often involves some medical history detective work.

This chapter outlines the history of rheumatic fever, including how it was discovered and efforts to treat and eliminate the condition.

Walter Cheadle, a prominent paediatrician and lecturer at St Mary's Hospital in London, was the first person to group symptoms that had previously seemed independent into one diagnosable condition: rheumatic fever. Given that it took until 1889 for Cheadle to make these connections, it is difficult to know how common rheumatic fever was prior to the twentieth century. Before Cheadle's lectures cemented medical thinking on the condition, the symptoms of rheumatic fever had fallen under the general rubric of 'rheumatism' – albeit a strange and unusual form, particularly when accompanied by cardiac symptoms. Clinicians debated throughout the 1800s exactly what this seemingly new condition was, and had difficulty settling on a name.[1]

During the American Civil War (1861–1865), 145,000 cases of 'acute rheumatism' were recorded, most of which are now thought to have been rheumatic fever.[2] Even in the decades following Cheadle's lectures, the true magnitude of the illnesses caused by *Streptococcus*, particularly *Group-A Strep*, remained underappreciated. During World War I, for instance, thousands of soldiers were admitted to hospitals with a condition called 'articular rheumatism', a diagnosis that implies that the primary symptoms were joint pains. Again, many of these cases may have been rheumatic fever.[3]

By 1910, the term rheumatic fever was sufficiently well-known to be used as an underlying cause of death, at least in the United States, where it was estimated that seven of every 100,000 deaths were caused by rheumatic fever (presumably severe rheumatic heart disease).[4] Still, these rates paled in comparison to that of its sister disease, scarlet fever, for which death rates in 1910 sat at around 25 per 100,000.[5] This difference in mortality rates could have been because scarlet fever was more common, or it could have been because, around 1910, rheumatic fever was more likely to go undiagnosed.

Rheumatic fever cases often went undocumented because it took time to accept the fundamental idea that a *Streptococcus* infection, or any other bacterial infection, could lead to a serious multi-system illness such as rheumatic fever. Despite microbiologist Rebecca Lancefield's painstaking work at the Rockefeller Institute in the 1920s and 1930s, where she described and classified *Streptococcus* bacteria in detail, the impact of these bacteria on public health wasn't yet fully understood, and the full range of possible symptoms of rheumatic fever remained unrecognised.[6] While the link between *Streptococcus* and rheumatic fever was being made throughout the 1930s,[7] the clearest evidence of the relationship emerged only during World War II when legions of American military service members contracted it.

In 1941, officials at three separate US Army training camps – Chanute Field and Scott Field in Illinois and Fort Knox in Kentucky – reported strange cases of scarlet fever.[8] In each case, patients suffered an initial illness with all the hallmarks of scarlet fever. Just as that sickness passed, a second one replaced it. This second illness shared many symptoms with the first, though with a brief remission period halfway through. The first and the second fevers differed in one striking way: the second was *not* accompanied by a scarlet rash. This raised the question of whether the two fevers were different illnesses altogether or serial manifestations of one disease.

In November 1941, a team of US Army physicians was dispatched to the camps to investigate these oddities. They discovered that, without exception, the camp's medical staff had little to no knowledge of the association between streptococcal infection and rheumatic fever. They also realised that rather than experiencing a strange, extended form of scarlet fever, the camps were actually having an outbreak of rheumatic fever.

As the war progressed, reports of rheumatic fever within the camps turned from a trickle to a flood.[9] In one severe outbreak in early 1943, at Fort Warren in Wyoming, the incidence of streptococcal infection hit 650 cases per 1000 soldiers: nearly seven out of every 10 soldiers. Over that same year, the US Army diagnosed almost 7000 patients with rheumatic fever within its camps. Most of the illnesses occurred in clusters, representing the close proximity of the patients. With so many soldiers out of commission at a crucial point in the war, the US Army began to take the risk posed by *Streptococcus* very seriously. By the end of the year, the US government had established a research programme dedicated to investigating the causes and possible treatment of rheumatic fever.

In 1943, using a technique developed shortly before the war, researchers tested a substance called sulfonamide, which had been shown to have antibacterial properties, to fight outbreaks of *Streptococcus* in three naval training schools. The results were dramatic. In the facilities where sulfonamide was trialled, rates of *Streptococcus*-related infection plummeted.[10] The military believed they had found an answer to the problem. Patients in other military camps experiencing outbreaks of rheumatic fever were dosed with sulfonamide, with similarly remarkable results.[11] Sulfonamide quickly became widely available in a range of antibacterial pharmaceuticals referred to as sulfa drugs. They were used, also in 1943, to successfully treat British Prime Minister Winston Churchill, who was suffering from severe pneumonia probably caused by a *Streptococcus pneumoniae* bacterial infection picked up while visiting troops in Tunisia.[12]

However, the success of sulfa drugs in treating streptococcal illnesses was fleeting. No sooner had sulfonamide dosing become an official military policy than reports surfaced that sulfonamide was no longer preventing outbreaks of rheumatic fever in the camps.[13] Researchers eventually discovered that those whom the sulfa drugs had failed to protect were infected with a new strain of *Streptococcus* that was resistant to sulfonamide. The face of the enemy had changed.

By the end of 1944, the usefulness of sulfonamide had peaked. Rates of both streptococcal infection and rheumatic fever in the military camps had reached epidemic levels, and by February 1945, the US Navy, Army and Air Force had largely abandoned the use of sulfa drugs.[14]

∽

During World War II, the movement of troops around the globe and their housing in crowded military camps provided an unparalleled opportunity in modern, biomedically sophisticated times to study infection and discover what causes infectious diseases to spread and thrive. Connections drawn by researchers in this period provided the first evidence of the relationship between living conditions and the spread of streptococcal diseases.

At the end of the war, US Army scientists published a paper showing how the movement of soldiers from a low-infection camp to a high-infection camp resulted in an immediate increase in streptococcal illness at the high-infection camp.[15] Most often, it was the troops who had made the transition to the new camp who fell ill, whereas those who had been stationed in the high-risk zone for more than six months appeared to be immune. The previously uninfected troops seemed to be providing fresh new host environments for the bacteria to colonise.

Army doctors who had visited the camps surmised that overcrowding within bunkrooms and classrooms was a major cause of streptococcal infection, as well as the subsequent outbreaks of rheumatic and scarlet fevers.[16] Still, the doctors faced the difficult task of proving their hunch because there was no such thing as a camp that *wasn't* overcrowded during the war. When occupied by troops, the military camps were jam-packed, and infection spread. When their occupants left to fight in Europe and the Pacific, illness rates invariably plummeted. It was impossible to conduct controlled experiments, and so a great opportunity to unequivocally establish the relationship between overcrowding and rheumatic fever development was lost. While the US Army doctors' hunch about the relationship between overcrowding and rheumatic fever would soon become accepted dogma, it would take more than half a century for that dogma to have evidence to support it.

∽

While the streptococcal epidemics were coursing through the camps, a physician named T. Duckett Jones began a research programme at the US Naval Training Station in Newport, Rhode Island. By 1941, Jones had developed a keen interest in *Streptococcus* and had researched its relationship to rheumatic fever. He was not entirely convinced that *Streptococcus* was the primary cause of rheumatic fever but did not try to discover alternative causes. Instead, he was among the early physicians who followed up on the sufferers of the illness and described what had happened to them *after* their diagnosis.

Cheadle, in 1889, had shown that carditis, chorea and polyarthritis (inflammation of multiple joints) were all symptoms of one 'syndrome': what he called the 'rheumatic state'.[17] In a 1944 article in the *Journal of the American Medical Association*, Jones further characterised the symptoms in a typical case of rheumatic fever.[18] He detailed the five major and seven minor symptoms that are common to rheumatic fever, with the ultimate aim of helping clinicians diagnose the disease. The major symptoms listed by Jones included heart inflammation (carditis), joint pain (arthralgia), jerky, involuntary movements (chorea), lumps or lesions under the skin (subcutaneous nodules), and rheumatic fever recurrence. The minor symptoms included fever, abdominal pain, chest pain, rashes, nosebleeds, pulmonary abnormalities and laboratory evidence of markers of inflammation.

Jones explained to his readership of eager clinicians that a combination of any two of the major indicators – or one major indicator plus at least one minor indicator, such as a high fever – was enough to make a reasonably confident diagnosis of rheumatic fever. Using Jones' criteria, Keg's 1969 experience becomes straightforward to diagnose. Keg had joint pain (arthralgia), signs of heart inflammation (carditis), and a high fever, alongside the high likelihood that the spotty throat he experienced after the West Auckland tournament was due to a *Group-A Strep* infection.

Jones' article was an instant classic in the field. At the time, clinicians were starving for anything that might help them diagnose this tricky condition. The criteria Jones proposed represented a leap forward in how the condition was diagnosed and, ultimately, treated. He had made the next logical move from Cheadle's work nearly 50 years earlier by pooling together the manifestations of the disease, in which one case can be strikingly different from the next, summarising its definitive characteristics and then providing his clinical colleagues with a diagnostic tool. Jones' sharpening of diagnostic technique and the subsequent standardisation of diagnosis throughout the clinical community enshrined his legacy as a warrior in the battle against rheumatic fever. The checklist of criteria used to diagnose the disease still bears his name. The current 'Modified Jones Criteria' remains largely unchanged from the original 1944 version.[19] In today's five major criteria, arthralgia has been replaced by polyarthritis (joint pain accompanied by inflammation), and erythema (a rare skin rash) replaces rheumatic fever recurrence. Among the minor criteria, joint pain without inflammation (polyarthralgia) has replaced abdominal or chest pain, while nosebleeds and pulmonary abnormalities are out, and heart wave abnormalities on an electrocardiogram (ECG) are in.

The Jones Criteria could not have been published at a more critical time. Between 1925 and 1950, rheumatic fever was the number one cause of death in American children between the ages of five and 19.[20] This shocking death rate among young people would have been due to the fever's fatal progress into rheumatic heart disease, making it the main cause of heart disease in Americans younger than 40. With the Jones Criteria, mid-twentieth-century doctors were able to diagnose a patient presenting with a host of disparate symptoms. Still, just because they could recognise symptoms did not mean they could improve patient outcomes. They still needed to discover how to prevent and treat rheumatic fever effectively.

With the effectiveness of sulfonamide against the streptococcal epidemics in army camps having waned so quickly, there was again no treatment for infection by these bacteria. However, while Jones and the US Army doctors were investigating rheumatic fever, a group of scientists in England had spent World War II working on a new chemical compound that showed great promise in destroying dangerous bacteria. This compound had been discovered more than a decade earlier, in 1928. The name of the discoverer was Alexander Fleming; the compound: penicillin.

∞

How Fleming discovered the antibacterial value of penicillin is the stuff of legend.[21] Returning to his London laboratory in September 1928 from a summer holiday, Fleming checked a stack of Petri dishes that contained *Staphylococcus* bacteria. He immediately noticed a strange fungus had grown in the middle of one of the dishes. Looking closer, he saw that the staphylococci surrounding the fungus were dead, their cell walls irreparably ruptured, while empty space separated the dead bacterial cells from the living. Something inside the fungus was causing the bacterial cell walls to split while also stopping the growth of the bacteria.

Of this pivotal moment, which would eventually save millions of lives, Fleming recorded drily: 'On a plate planted with staphylococci a colony of mould appeared. After about two weeks it was seen that the colonies of staphylococci near the mould colony were degenerate.'[22]

Some of the details of this story are disputed. The timeline, from plating the bacteria to the growth of the penicillin, as reported by Fleming, is rather convenient, and the circumstantial factors don't quite add up, including the now-debunked notion that the mould grew from a spore that flew in through an open window. But it remains undisputed that Fleming had discovered an organism that inhibited the growth of and killed *Staphylococcus*.

It took years before the treatment of bacterial infections with penicillin gained momentum as a lifesaving intervention. At least some of this inertia was due to Fleming's own failures when it came to documenting and communicating his findings. He was a brilliant scientist but a poor salesman. His first presentation at London's Medical Research Club in 1929 was so self-deprecating that those present at the meeting doubted the importance of his message. When he asked for questions from the audience, he was met with silence. (Fleming would later refer to this presentation as 'that frightful moment'.) Later that year, he published his findings in the *British Journal of Experimental Pathology*. Summing up his findings, he wrote, 'It has been demonstrated that a species of penicillium produces in culture a very powerful antibacterial substance which affects different bacteria in different degrees.' He also noted, 'Penicillin is non-toxic to animals in enormous doses and is [a] non-irritant'.[23] Establishing that penicillin was safe for animals was crucial if it was to have any hope of medical application.

Eventually, Fleming's 1929 manuscript would be celebrated as a pivotal paper that began a new era in the fight against streptococcal disease, and Fleming would be lauded as the father of the antibiotic revolution. For many years, however, his voice went unheard. Penicillin needed champions to advance Fleming's discovery and demonstrate its importance to medicine.

∽

During the 1930s, a group of scientists at Oxford University, led by the Australian Howard Florey, worked to turn penicillin into a therapeutic tool.[24] By 1939, they had isolated the purest form of penicillin – a step that had eluded others in the years since Fleming's discovery – and in 1940 they demonstrated that penicillin was effective against *Group-A Strep*, though initially only in mice.

In the early years of World War II they began testing penicillin on human subjects. First, they needed to validate Fleming's claim and ensure that the medicine was not toxic to humans. Elva Akers, a 50-year-old woman dying of breast cancer in a local hospital, volunteered to be a human research subject, even after Florey's team explained that the medicine would do nothing to cure her cancer.[25] The team delivered the medicine into Akers' bloodstream and monitored her for serious side effects. There were none. She died of her cancer shortly after the experiment, a hero in the fight against streptococcal illness.

The team also needed to prove that penicillin was as effective against *Streptococcus* in humans as it had been in mice. So, in 1941, they visited the local hospital's septic ward to look for candidates. A middle-aged policeman named Albert Alexander had scratched his face while gardening and had developed a bad infection that had claimed his left eye. His lungs and shoulder had also become infected, and he had developed sepsis that threatened to shut down his organs. Alexander agreed to receive a dose of penicillin and to be observed as it circulated through his body, fighting the infection. He was given a large first dose, followed by another three smaller doses over the next 12 hours. Then the patient and physicians waited.

Within a day, Alexander returned from the brink of death. His temperature was normal, and his inflammation had receded. Within five days, he was sitting up and eating. Just 10 days after the first dose, it seemed he was headed for a full recovery.

Still, Florey's team was in unknown medical territory. The immediate improvement was encouraging, but given the extent of Alexander's trauma, the penicillin's effect would need to last long enough for his body to reverse the damage. The team was unsure how long they needed to administer the new medicine. Did they keep giving it until Alexander showed signs of lasting improvement, or until all the bacteria were gone? With penicillin in short supply, the team simply did not have enough to properly treat the patient. To get around this problem, Florey ordered that regular urine samples be taken from Alexander, since about 80 percent of each dose of penicillin administered would be excreted this way from his body. At its laboratory, the team harvested penicillin from Alexander's urine and prepared it for redeployment.

Sadly, the volume of penicillin wasn't enough to have a lasting effect. After the 10 day 'honeymoon phase', his condition quickly deteriorated as sepsis returned. Soon after, his lungs and other organs capitulated. He died a few weeks later. But an important point had been made. Here was a patient in linear decline with a raging bacterial infection who had responded dramatically to treatment. If more penicillin had been available, Florey's team might have saved Albert Alexander's life. Buoyed by his case, Florey and his team experimented further.

Before long, they had an effective and stable compound ready for mass production. Large-scale manufacturing was organised through a series of perilous Atlantic journeys between Oxford and the United States. By 1942, word of penicillin's efficacy had spread, and pharmaceutical companies such as Merck and Pfizer were working together on mass production as part of the war effort. By the time of the Normandy landings in June 1944, pharmaceutical companies were making enough penicillin to treat 40,000 cases of streptococcal infection a month.[26]

Fleming and Florey had shown that penicillin was a powerful antagonist of *Group-A Strep*, and by the mid-twentieth century, this antagonistic interaction had been deployed to prevent serious illness and save lives. A month after the end of World War II, in October 1945, Florey and his partner Ernst Chain, along with Alexander Fleming, received the Nobel Prize. Together, they had brought about a new era in the fight against bacterial infection. The age of antibiotics had begun.

Chapter Four
Gone, not gone

BY THE TIME OF KEG'S ILLNESS in 1969, penicillin use for the treatment of rheumatic fever had become routine. Keg's doctor started him on a course of oral penicillin as soon as he found the pus-filled spots at the back of his throat. The antibiotics travelled in Keg's bloodstream around his body. At the infection site in Keg's throat, penicillin attached themselves to the cell wall of each *Group-A Strep* bacterium. The penicillin caused a breach in the bacterial cell wall, allowing surrounding fluid to leak into the *Group-A Strep* cell, swelling it until it burst.

Penicillin destroyed as many bacteria as it could and then left Keg's body. After an hour or two, most of the dose he had taken was eliminated through his kidneys, in his urine. Regular dosing was needed to keep the battle going. In 1941, Florey and his team had been unable to dose often enough to prevent Albert Alexander's septicaemic death. By the 1960s, mass production of the medication had overcome this problem. Why, then, did Keg's symptoms worsen, even after days on penicillin?

The answer is that *Group-A Strep* was no longer causing Keg's symptoms. The penicillin had quickly mopped up whatever *Group-A*

Strep remained at the rear of his throat, but the strong cascade of immune system reactions that would forever alter Keg's life had already begun. His painful wrists, ankles and knees were a major clue to what was happening within his body. What had started as a 'strep throat' was now an autoimmune illness affecting multiple sites and body systems: Keg had developed rheumatic fever. Specifically, as well as a high fever and joint pains, he had developed cardiac symptoms pointing to carditis, the inflammation that could cause permanent damage to his heart tissue. This permanent damage is what characterises the condition known as rheumatic heart disease. The *Group-A Strep* infection may have loaded and cocked the pistol, but it was his immune system that pulled the trigger.

This raises the question of why penicillin is given at all if it is obvious that a patient is suffering from full-blown rheumatic fever. Eradicating the remaining *Group-A Strep* in a person with rheumatic fever is not done to cure their immediate condition. Rather, because having had rheumatic fever once makes a person more susceptible to future attacks, penicillin is given to stave off new *Group-A Strep* infections. Its use is largely prophylactic, in the way the US soldiers in high-risk army bases in the 1940s were given sulfa drugs. In the presence of penicillin, *Group-A Strep* doesn't have a chance to gain a foothold. So, in 1969, to prevent another *Group-A Strep* infection, Keg started on a long course of oral penicillin, remaining on it for a year.[1]

These days, a patient like Keg would receive monthly penicillin injections directly into a large muscle for a minimum of 10 years.[2] This is a painful procedure, and the commitment required in terms of time and fortitude is a hefty burden to inflict on a (usually) young person. It's done because the benefit of possibly preventing a repeated bout of the illness – with all the associated risks to the heart and joints – outweighs any potential harm.

Historically, penicillin dramatically altered the fight against rheumatic fever, substantially reducing the risk of recurrence in those areas where the disease was commonplace. However, in North America and the United Kingdom, a decline in rheumatic fever rates predated the introduction of penicillin by decades.[3] Penicillin may have been a crucial leap forward in rheumatic fever treatment and prevention, but it did not lead to its overall decline. Even in the twenty-first century, we do not fully understand what did. It will not be possible to define the reason or reasons for the drop in cases until we can explain adequately what causes rheumatic fever in the first place.

∽

In developed countries, conditions caused by *Group-A Strep* once presented a deep societal crisis. In the late 1920s, for instance, a full quarter of the beds in New York City hospitals were filled with people suspected of suffering from the condition that was increasingly known as rheumatic fever.[4] At some hospitals, entire hospital wards were dedicated to treating its symptoms. Yet, within a matter of decades, the wards emptied. Throughout the early- to mid-twentieth century (with some exceptions, as we shall see) the disease had been all but eliminated from those countries where it had been rife.

Our understanding of why this rapid decline happened is limited by the scarcity of good data. Few people or organisations systematically collected information on how common rheumatic fever was, and those in the field did not know what to look for. Jones did not draw up his criteria until the mid-1940s, and until then, diagnosing rheumatic fever was more art than science.

The data that do exist give us the broad brushstrokes of the disease's evolution.[5] In the late 1800s in Copenhagen, when the understanding of rheumatic fever (and use of that name) was still relatively new, the case rate was estimated to be 200 people for every

100,000. After that, the rates abruptly tumbled. By 1930, rates were down to 100 cases per 100,000. By 1960, there were only around 10 cases per 100,000. England, Wales and the United States had similar patterns.

Rheumatic fever rates dropped even further in the latter half of the twentieth century.[6] Between 1960 and 1980, the number of cases in the United States decreased from 10–20 cases per 100,000 to barely one case per 100,000. Along with this substantial drop came a sharp reduction in mortality, with deaths dropping from seven per 100,000 people in the United States to close to zero by the end of the 1970s. Rheumatic fever was not the only streptococcal illness to retreat.[7] Deaths from scarlet fever plummeted from more than 200 per 100,000 children in England and Wales around 1900 to practically zero by the 1950s.

Why the abrupt decline? The reasons are still not clear. With rheumatic fever, the evidence we have suggests that a combination of individual and environmental factors led to the drop in cases. Such factors include changes in housing, nutrition and medical care during the mid-twentieth century. Yet the beneficial effects of these kinds of improvements have not been evenly distributed across all communities living in developed countries. As we will return to later, in New Zealand rheumatic fever remains a common disease, but only for members of a few particular communities. Understanding the factors behind the near disappearance of rheumatic fever from other developed countries might provide some vital clues for how to address these disparities and eliminate the disease once and for all.

∽

By the 1840s, when Ignaz Semmelweis discovered the prophylactic value of handwashing with chlorine, the Industrial Revolution had produced a large middle class.[8] Many in the West now had enough money to escape unhealthy living conditions. Grimy, overcrowded apartments still existed, but far fewer people lived in them. This meant fewer people were exposed to the conditions that are most conducive to streptococcal proliferation. Meanwhile, advances in medical research, such as Pasteur's germ theory, had led to a fundamental shift in how disease was conceptualised and treated. Instead of viewing ourselves as passive victims of 'miasma', germ theory showed us that we could fight and win against infectious disease. In developed countries, this higher standard of living and better quality of medical care probably led to a significant reduction overall in *Group-A Strep* disease. By extension, rates of rheumatic fever fell in regions where the disease had previously been common.

Beyond the standard of living and medical care, what other changes across the twentieth century could have caused the abrupt decline in rates of rheumatic fever in developed countries?

Genetic research suggests that certain gene expressions may influence a person's risk of developing rheumatic fever.[9] However, the rapid decline in rheumatic fever rates appears more likely to have been caused by significant improvements in living conditions than genetic changes in the susceptible population.[10] This does not rule out the possibility that the interaction between a person's genetic makeup and environmental factors is important.

Nutrition is another factor to consider. During the twentieth century, advances in agriculture made a wide range of foods more available to the general population. Accordingly, one theory is that better nutrition may have made us more resistant to streptococcal disease.[11] Again, though, there is insufficient evidence that general improvements in diet were responsible for the decline in the disease.[12] As American doctor and infectious disease researcher Edward Kass observed in the early 1970s, only extreme nutritional deficiencies would make a person more susceptible to streptococcal infection.

A curious feature of rheumatic fever today is that it predominantly affects children between the ages of five and 14 years old.[13] This correlation between age and initial diagnosis is so strong that a person presenting with symptoms of rheumatic fever as an adult is assumed to have had a previous attack as a child. It is possible, then, that many of the US soldiers and marines who contracted rheumatic fever in the military camps of the 1940s had previously had it in childhood – although, since medical history of rheumatic fever was not systematically recorded in these soldiers at this time, we will never know whether or not this was the case.

Why does the disease usually manifest in children? For starters, children are very likely to be exposed to *Group-A Strep*, whether at daycare, school, or just playing with their friends. The current best guess about why this can lead to rheumatic fever is that a child's young and blossoming immune system is vulnerable to manipulation by *Streptococcus*, causing it to 'overreact' in an attempt to outwit the bacteria.[14] The older we get, the 'wiser' our immune system becomes, reducing the likelihood of an exaggerated immune response to streptococcal infection.

Somewhat paradoxically, it is also thought that a child's immune system needs to have had at least some exposure to *Group-A Strep* in order to precipitate the chain of events that leads to rheumatic fever. There is a hypothesis that multiple *Group-A Strep* infections over time throw the immune system's checks and balances into disarray and launch it into self-attacking aggression, a defense called 'immune priming' that backfires on itself.[15] The basic idea is that children might successfully fight off several infections with immune responses, but then reach a tipping point.

With these factors in mind, could the swift decline in rates of rheumatic fever be related to changes in the age of susceptibility to the disease? For this to be the case, there would have had to be a similarly rapid change in our immune systems' readiness to react to the strains of streptococci in circulation. In other words, our immune system would have needed to become exponentially smarter, or *Streptococcus* exponentially dumber – and both scenarios are a little far-fetched. The human immune system could not have evolved so much in a century that it has learned to deal with *Group-A Strep* much earlier in life. Therefore, it seems implausible that age at diagnosis is a factor in the steep decline in rheumatic fever.

Evidence that the bacteria have rapidly evolved is also weak. The notion that rates of rheumatic fever dropped because of changes in the strains of *Streptococcus* in dominant circulation has been largely refuted.[16] A group of researchers in Chicago did find that the types of *Group-A Strep* prevalent today are different from those most common around the time Keg fell ill.[17] However, with more than 200 strains and sub-strains of *Group-A Strep*, dominant strains are likely to change over time. It is safe to conclude that the remarkable decline in rates of rheumatic fever in the twentieth century was unlikely to have been due to some major shift in the strains of *Group-A Strep* that our immune system encountered.

In summary, neither we nor *Group-A Strep* could have changed enough over the nineteenth and twentieth centuries to explain the dramatic reduction in rheumatic fever. This leaves us with the theory that the disease was unable to flourish due to societal changes, such as improved living conditions. But, as the next chapter will show, determining which societal factors were most responsible for the downturn is not straightforward. Nevertheless, we can make one consistent observation from the available data: rheumatic fever rates are tied to socioeconomic conditions.

∽

Around the time of Keg's rheumatic fever diagnosis in 1969, disease patterns in New Zealand were similar to those in the rest of the world.[18] For most New Zealanders, the risk of rheumatic fever had declined.

However, as early as the 1950s, there was evidence showing significant disparities in the incidence of rheumatic fever between countries of differing economic development and within the borders of individual countries. While rates of the disease may have fallen for the majority of people around the world, things were not as bright for some minority groups. Moreover, once the incidence of rheumatic fever was measured in regions where it had previously gone undocumented, the theory that rheumatic fever was heading for extinction began to founder.

Data on the incidence of rheumatic fever in developing countries over the twentieth century are scant, but they do reveal this contrasting portrait of the disease. While in the United States rheumatic fever cases dropped to around 10 to 20 per 100,000 people by the 1950s,[19] case numbers were much higher farther south. In Peru, the rate of rheumatic fever cases per 100,000 was around 30,[20] while in Costa Rica it was 120.[21] By the 1960s, the rate in Sri Lanka was 110 per 100,000,[22] while in the Pacific, cases among the Indian population of Fiji were around 140 per 100,000.[23] At the same time, rates in Nordic regions such as Denmark and Sweden were closer to one per 100,000.[24]

In New Zealand, there are significant disparities in rheumatic fever rates by socioeconomic status and by ethnicity. Of the cases of rheumatic fever diagnosed in New Zealand, nine out of 10 occur among Māori or Pacific peoples. Māori are around 30 times more likely to develop rheumatic fever than New Zealand Europeans.[25] Pacific New Zealanders are around 40 times more likely. Consequently, rates of rheumatic heart disease are three to five times higher among Māori and Pacific peoples compared to New Zealand

Europeans. This disparity has grown by around 25 percent over the last two decades.[26]

As in New Zealand, stark differences in regard to rheumatic fever exist among ethnic groups in Australia.[27] Despite making up less than five percent of the population, Indigenous Australians account for around 95 percent of Australia's cases of rheumatic fever. The number of new rheumatic fever cases among Indigenous Australians has increased by 40 percent in the last five years. They are now around 96 times more likely to develop rheumatic fever than non-Indigenous Australians. The strong pattern of disease by ethnicity in Australia and New Zealand is unlikely to have anything to do with genetics, but rather differences in the experience of environmental factors (such as poor living conditions) that drive exposure to *Group-A Strep*.[28]

The extreme divergence in cases of rheumatic fever between developed and developing countries, and within developed countries such as New Zealand and Australia, is cause for considerable concern. The burden of this disease is clearly not shared equally, and the ramifications of this inequity are profound. Rheumatic fever is a condition that occurs most commonly in children living in deprivation and in marginalised populations, frequently leaving permanent marks. The legacy of the disease can return, disastrously, in adulthood.

Chapter Five
The long shadow

WINTER, 2004

2:27am
The clock on the dashboard of my Honda sedan glows neon green as we race down East Tamaki Drive in South Auckland. Rain has left deep puddles over which we hydroplane. I'm going too fast on tyres that should have been replaced long ago, but I've got no choice.

'Floor it, mate.'

Dad is leaning back in the passenger seat with his eyes closed. He says those words delicately, as though he's begging rather than telling. He's not in control of the car. He's barely in control of his own body.

It's the third time in as many months that Dad and I are bound for the Middlemore Hospital emergency room. It's early Saturday morning — the worst possible time to go to the emergency room in South Auckland.

2:28am
I have none of Dad's wet-weather driving skills. He'd raced Holden Commodores well into his 60s all around New Zealand. So I ignore

his plea for more speed. Instead, I just pat his leg and tell him everything is going to be all right. I don't know if it will be. I'm not really talking to him, anyway. I'm trying to convince myself.

About 20 minutes earlier, my sleep had been broken by a loud knock on my bedroom door. Then Mum had walked into my room and turned on my light. Dad's heart was playing up again, she said, and he thought it was a bad one. Could I please take him to hospital?

Of course I could. When Dad was in hospital, there wasn't any place I would rather have been than by his side. I hated it, of course. I hated every moment, sometimes so much that I fantasised about crawling out of the ward through a vent in the ceiling. But not knowing if he was alive or dead was far worse. You can't relax when your Superman is confronting his version of kryptonite.

So I had jumped out of bed, dressed and helped Dad to the car. Whenever this happened, he tried to put on a brave face, but his body language betrayed him. If he was talking really fast, it meant he had tachycardia (a rapid heartbeat) and couldn't bring it under control. If his speech was slow and slurring, it meant that his heart wasn't beating enough to give his brain the blood it needed. He could be as stoic as he liked, but his physiology would reveal the truth.

We were on the road five minutes later. His stoic demeanour vanished. 'Get there as soon as you can, mate. It's a bad one.'

We had learned it was much quicker for me to drive Dad to the hospital than to wait for an ambulance. South Auckland is so vast you could never predict how long an ambulance would take. After we had experienced a few desperately long waits, we decided that it was quickest for me to just get him there myself.

It had been pouring with rain when we'd left home, and our combined breath fogged up the windscreen. It was going to be a sketchy drive.

2:39am

As East Tamaki Drive ends, we wait to turn onto Great South Road. The road is empty, and only the rhythmic tick-tock of the indicator breaks the silence. Every second we wait for the red light to turn green feels like an hour. Dad opens his eyes when he realises the car has stopped. Realising we aren't at the hospital, he mumbles:

'Just run it, mate … please.'

As I poke the Honda's nose into the middle of the intersection, the lights for Great South Road turn orange.

When I was a boy, Dad had taught me to impress passengers by knowing when the red traffic light would turn green. Dad did it all the time, and one day he revealed his secret. Pulling up to a red light at an intersection, he told me to look at the light that was currently green. 'When it turns orange, count backwards from five.' He explained that all the traffic lights were on timers, and there was always a five-second gap between one light turning orange and the next light in the sequence turning green. Once you had worked out the light sequence for a given intersection, you were all set to wow your passengers. I used this trick as a teen many times to impress my female passengers. One of them married me.

As soon as the Great South Road light flashes orange, I start counting. Five. Four. Three. Two.

One.

At zero, I turn.

'Floor it, mate … *please.*'

We speed down Great South Road and then onto Shirley Road.

Even 20 years later, I can still remember the street names. Turn off Shirley Road and take a right onto Swaffield Road, which runs into Hospital Road. I'd become so used to driving that route that once, on the way to a different hospital on the other side of South Auckland for a research meeting, I had automatically driven to Middlemore.

I didn't realise my error until I had pulled up to the emergency room and realised I didn't have Dad to drop off.

This time, Dad was in the car, and we parked beneath the bright red sign to the emergency room and shuffled inside. Since it was the witching hour on a Saturday morning, the foyer resembled the entrance to a prison, not a healthcare facility. There seemed to be as many tall and well-muscled security guards as orderlies, and the triage nurse behind the reception desk stood shielded behind a transparent plastic wall.

I could tell Dad's anxiety was lifting. Just being in the same building as someone who had the skills to fix him gave him a renewed sense of hope. He even walked up to the desk as casually as if he were paying for petrol. I wanted to take over – to at least fill out the forms – but I think Dad had decided I had done my job already. The only people who could help him now were on the other side of those double doors behind the reception desk.

He told me to move the car from blocking the emergency room doors. I wanted to stay with him, but he tried to assure me he would be fine, and we would need the car to get home once they had fixed him up. He was right. The car would be no good to us if towed away.

I could not argue with Dad. He is the most cheerful man I know. He does not get angry. He gets powerfully exasperated. Dad's version of a heated dressing-down is his right hand rubbing his temple. I wasn't about to add to his emotional burden, so I just nodded.

When I got to the door, I turned to look at Dad. He was still standing at the reception desk, leaning on his elbows, explaining his symptoms as clearly as he could to the nurse at the night window.

∞

These events repeated themselves many times throughout my teens and early twenties. Only once I had moved into a flat with my then-girlfriend, now wife, did the midnight shuttles down East Tamaki Drive stop. Since I wasn't around, and because my mum had to stay home with my sister Nicole, who has a disability, calling an ambulance became the most efficient way to get Dad to hospital. I would still get a text from Mum to let me know that he was in an ambulance and that I shouldn't worry; there was nothing I could do about it anyway. Often I'd throw on jeans and a jacket, and meet the ambulance at the hospital. In the years when the ambulance trips became more frequent, I'd sometimes take Mum's advice and guiltily go back to bed and try to pretend it wasn't happening.

My experience in those years was not unique. Thousands of families across New Zealand and millions around the world grapple with the same thing: the lifelong consequences of a childhood illness. I've called this chapter 'the long shadow' because rheumatic heart disease tethers rheumatic fever sufferers to their illness for the rest of their (probably shortened) lives. At every doctor's appointment, they will be the subject of increased scrutiny and curiosity. The stethoscope will linger a little longer on their chests as the doctor searches for a murmur. The doctor will suggest that it's time for another ultrasound to see how the valve is doing, and how long it might last. The conversation will then turn to the six different medicines that are keeping the disease in check: two to maintain the cardiac rhythm, two to steady the blood pressure, one to cut the bad cholesterol and one to stop the vomiting caused by the other five not mixing well.

And that's just for those who have access to good healthcare. Those without fare much worse.

Still, despite the constant physical reminders of their condition, sufferers can lead a normal adult life. Keg, for example, is a testament to this. Before he became a father, he'd been a guitar-toting high school hunk, and he played in the Hora Hora premier club rugby team in Whangārei for years. He would have likely played halfback for Northland if his rugby career hadn't intersected with that of Northland and All Black legend Sid Going. No other halfback in the country – let alone Whangārei – had a chance against Super Sid.

Dad ran marathons and managed successful businesses, including a frozen food company that was growing fast when my sister suffered severe encephalopathy. He then spent over a decade helping my sister walk and talk. The talking never came, but through hard work and my parents' devotion, she eventually walked. I don't know where Dad got the energy to do all this.

Toward the end of the 1980s, the dark stains of rheumatic fever's long shadow began to surface in Dad. We would often find him napping in the middle of the day. He'd deny he was sleeping; he was 'just resting his eyes'. He was a heroic napper. We would joke that he could sleep through a nuclear apocalypse and then wake up wondering where everyone had gone.

The reason behind the naps was serious. Dad's heart was beginning to show the signs of damage typical of rheumatic heart disease. He was tired because the blood flow to his brain wasn't sufficient. He was tired because his heart worked harder than a non-diseased heart. He was tired because he'd had rheumatic fever, and the darkness of that childhood illness obscured the light of his future.

∽

To understand what rheumatic heart disease is and why it manifests in adulthood, let's return again to 1969 and the moment that Keg's immune system reacted to the *Group-A Strep* at the back of his throat. *Group-A Strep* can escape detection and destruction in many ways, but mimicry is its main strategy.

Think of mimicry as camouflage.[1] Just like a soldier donning green fatigues in a jungle, part of the *Group-A Strep* cell mimics the shape and appearance of its new surroundings. In this way, the bacteria hide from the immune system. Meanwhile the immune system, having been alerted that something isn't right, is actively on the lookout for unusual cells.

The camouflage assumed by the *Group-A Strep* cell makes it resemble cells in our brains, skin, joints and hearts. In an autoimmune response typical of a serious case of rheumatic fever, our immune system sees through the camouflage, correctly identifying *Group-A Strep* as the invader that it is. However, it then goes on searching for anything else that looks like *Group-A Strep* and, once found, launches the same kind of attack that it would use to combat a bacterial infection. The result is that instead of a stealth mission that captures and destroys only the camouflaged enemy battalion, our immune system burns down the whole jungle.

Mimicry is the crucial link between what is a relatively simple bacterial infection and the significant long-term consequences it can have for the body. Mimicry created the conduit connecting Keg's throat to his heart. If *Group-A Strep* did not engage in mimicry, a wayward autoimmune response would not occur. There would be no painful joints and no swollen hearts. Instead, in a serious case of rheumatic fever, cardiac tissue can become so acutely inflamed by the immune response that normal heart function is seriously impaired, to the point of heart failure.[2] Typically, cardiac swelling is moderate and requires only sustained bed rest for the inflammation to recede. That would be the end of the problem, if not for our fragile heart valves.

∞

I've always found cardiac anatomy captivating. I am amazed by this constant pump, sitting right in my chest, without which all other systems would instantly crumble. I'm fascinated by the brilliant simplicity of the heart's architecture. One side collects blood that needs oxygen and pumps it to the lungs. The other receives oxygen-rich blood back from the lungs and pushes it out to the rest of the body. The upper chambers on each side holding blood in a waiting room of sorts are aptly called the atria. The two chambers on the bottom are the ventricles that pump blood away from the heart, to the lungs and into the circulatory system. Day and night, that ceaseless thumping in our chests goes with us.

Heart valves play a major role in the effective functioning of the heart. Made of a special type of tissue, they regulate blood flow through the heart's chambers and direct it out via the aortic artery for circulation throughout the body, or via the pulmonary artery for blood heading to the lungs. I learned about heart valves during a lab for one of my undergraduate anatomy papers. My lab partner and I dissected a cow heart, which is like a human heart but much bigger (and easier to obtain since donated human hearts were reserved for postgraduate students). We sliced open the heart to reveal its chambers, and there they were: a perfectly preserved pair of valves, like swinging gates between the cow's left atrium and left ventricle.

These 'gates' were connected to the inside of the bottom chamber by a stringy web of tissue, as if Spiderman had sprayed his webbing between the heart wall and valves. These were the *chordae tendinae* – the 'heart strings' that stop the gates from standing ajar and letting blood flow backwards into the atrium. If blood flowed backwards to the atrium, the ventricles would have less to pump around the body. I used my scalpel to cut through one of the cords. It snapped and folded back against the wall. I found this oddly satisfying, so I cut another – and another – until one valve was completely separated from the ventricle and moving slightly in the current of the laboratory's air conditioning.

As soon as I had sliced through that last bit of connective tissue, I realised the valve was the bit of the heart that was broken on Dad.

Until that moment, I hadn't seen the relationship between what I was doing in the lab and what was happening to him. I had been absentmindedly fiddling with the same tissue that had brought pain to our family and many others. I guiltily handed the scalpel to my lab partner for her to continue the dissection.

The ease with which I had severed those heart strings perfectly illustrates the fragile condition of our valves and their vital cardiac role. Their design is as exquisite as it is delicate. The cardiac inflammation caused by a bad case of rheumatic fever may leave the valve severely damaged, which, over time, will lead to irregularities of blood flow between the chambers. Without, or sometimes in spite of, medical intervention, this damage can lead to heart failure and death.

∽

My father's overall good health during his late youth and early adulthood coincided with the 'clinically silent' phase of his rheumatic heart disease.[3] The damage he had sustained as a child to the valve between his left atrium and his left ventricle could still be seen by ultrasound, but its effect was virtually undetectable, apart from the quiet murmur only his doctor could hear.

That murmur was the signal that his valve was not shutting properly and that blood was flowing between his chambers, rather than in one direction. The cords connecting his valves to his ventricles had been stretched during his clash with rheumatic fever and had lost most of their vital tension. With each beat, Dad's heart leaked a little, 60 times a minute, 86,000 times a day, 600,000 times a week. And that was Keg's heart pumping when he wasn't running a marathon or chasing Sid Going.

As the 1980s yielded to the 1990s, the constant regurgitation of blood began to take a toll. Just as a steady drip can wear away rock over time, Keg's heart's structure began to change in order to compensate for the persistent leaking.[4] To make up for the slight decrease in the volume of blood pumped with each beat, his heart had to work even harder to push blood to the rest of his body, which, over time, would increase the size of his heart and raise his blood pressure. High blood pressure would lead to disruptions in the flow of blood through his heart. All of these distorted flow dynamics increased the risk of a blood clot forming within his heart. If it travelled to his brain, that clot would cause a stroke. As well as needing blood pressure medication at around the age of 30, Dad also needed blood thinners. This meant every shaving cut gushed. A deep wound could be life-threatening.

The changes in his blood flow and heart structure were only part of Keg's problem. After a dozen years of beating 3600 wonky times an hour, his heart's electrical wiring began to play up. Rather than being led by one natural pacemaker, the sinoatrial node just above the two atrial chambers, Dad's heart fired electrical signals at random times. It began with a few irregular beats here and there. Eventually, these beats would become trills and wonky scales leaving Dad breathless. One night, after a particularly strong coffee, Dad's heart kicked up a syncopated rhythm that would not stop.

∾

This was my father's first bout of atrial fibrillation, a condition in which the heart's lead pacemaker ceases to be the only source of the spark that spreads electricity through the heart.[5] A single source is crucial because it ensures that the muscle cells around our heart contract at the right time. A fraction too early and the heart will contract too soon; a fraction too late and the contraction will be delayed. Having the lead pacemaker above the two atrial chambers means the muscle cells in the atrium will contract first to push the last bit of blood down into the ventricle, followed by the ventricle muscle, which pushes blood away from the heart and into the circulatory system.

Atrial fibrillation is an electrical storm in the heart. The lead pacemaker is no longer completely in charge. Rather, new signals crackle from cells within the atrium, disrupting the heart's rhythm. The result is a symphony without a conductor: the atrium beats independent of the ventricle, and coordination between the two chambers is lost. The blood supply pumped out of the heart drops because the atrium isn't filling the ventricle properly. Blood flow within the heart is also turbulent. Anyone suffering from atrial fibrillation feels weak, tired and light-headed. The danger of blood clots forming, and therefore of stroke or death, rises.

Dad described his experience of atrial fibrillation as a rushing sensation, as though a fast-forward button had been pressed and there was nothing he could do to stop it. Our midnight trips to Middlemore Hospital were almost always due to his suffering from this condition. The rushing feeling he experienced came from his chaotic heartbeats, which would patter at around 180 beats per minute, then suddenly dip down to 40, or even 30. His heart did this all day and all night until it found the right rhythm on its own, which was rare, or a doctor intervened.

While atrial fibrillation is awful, the intervention can seem equally so. A procedure known as cardioversion is one of the most common ways to alleviate atrial fibrillation. Cardioversion is a bit like turning a recalcitrant computer off and then restarting it again. It involves using defibrillator paddles, the ones that look like the diminutive clothes irons that you see on TV medical shows when a doctor yells 'CLEAR!' before zapping a patient. The goal is to restore the heart's natural rhythm by delivering a sudden jolt of electricity to a person's heart. This overrides the malfunctioning electrical impulses and resets the system. The physician stops the heart, and then the body's natural pacemaker starts it again. The hope is that when the heart resumes beating, the former faulty rhythm has been replaced by a normal one.

Blasting the heart with electricity is risky. On the one hand, a jolt might do nothing, and the heart rhythm will remain chaotic. On the other hand, the sudden charge can also cause the heart to release any blood clots it harbours into the brain, resulting in stroke or death.

In the Middlemore Hospital emergency room with my father, I would compulsively keep an eye on his monitor. I hated being in that room, and I hated the monitors even more, with their innocent chirps every time his heart rate rose too high or dipped too low, their flashing lights indicating a blood pressure of 220/130. I wanted to hug the nurse who recognised the pointlessness of the beeps and boops and eventually turned the sound off. At least then I could keep an eye on Dad in peace.

In silence I would focus on his body, the rise and fall of his chest. He tried to control his heart rate through slow and steady breathing, but the erratic shuddering of his beating heart that sent ripples across his lower rib cage would betray him. The contractions of his heart rattled his ribs with each messy beat. I didn't need to look at his monitor; I could have drawn an approximate ECG just from observing the contours of those ripples.

If he had enough time before leaving for the emergency room, Dad would grab his Discman or iPod (depending on the decade) from his bedside drawer. At the hospital, he would put headphones on to slow down or at least ease the rush. Sometimes he'd play The Eagles, maybe 'Peaceful Easy Feeling'. Usually, he played Pink Floyd. I often heard Dave Gilmour's soaring guitar above the awful chirps of the monitors.

Cardioversion would eventually return Dad's heart to its accustomed rhythm. After a few days of feeling extremely fragile and wary, as if his torment might start again at any moment, he would begin to feel normal again. After a week, he'd be back to his usual self, and my family and I once more began to take his seemingly stable health for granted.

∽

Around the age of 55, Keg's cardiologist decided it was time for a more long-term solution. He enlisted the help of a clinical colleague, a cardiac surgeon who specialised in a technique called cardiac ablation surgery. At first blush, the procedure sounds like it was designed by a madman. The surgeon inserts a small probe into the veins around the heart. The probe contains wires through which the surgeon begins to send electrical stimulation. The in-turn electrical response from the heart to the stimulation is then closely monitored for abnormal responses. The surgeon is looking for aberrance; electrical signals that are out of step with the main rhythm. When the surgeon finds the culprit, they use the equivalent of a soldering iron to zap the offending cells, creating scar tissue. The process is then repeated all over again, until all the cells with poor rhythm are zapped, replaced by new walls of scar tissue.

For Dad and our family, this procedure was a scary step into the unknown. The cardioversions had become routine and, while frightening, the result was at least predictable. However, we all knew that the frequent trips to the defibrillator were not sustainable. We also knew that they would become more dangerous as Dad got older. The ablation procedure was a no-brainer.

I still vividly remember the day of his first ablation surgery. (Spoiler: like all surgery, cardiac ablation often buys time rather than certainty.) I remember driving him into Mercy Hospital in Auckland, searching for anything to talk about other than the thing that I was driving him toward. I remember thinking that I needed to make a note of everything we were talking about in case they were some of our last words to each other. In retrospect, it was a silly thing to think.

In the moment, with all the uncertainty of the novel procedure, it didn't seem so silly.

I remember standing beside Dad in the plush reception area – The Ritz compared to the emergency department at Middlemore – while he casually chatted to the receptionist and checked himself in. Because he had been recently cardioverted back into normal rhythm, Dad was feeling perfectly fine. I remember sitting opposite him in the waiting room, knowing I would soon have to leave him to it. Occasionally, fear about the procedure would grip me, and I would internally question whether he needed to go through with it at all. More than once I thought about whisking him out of the waiting room and away from the soldering iron.

Eventually a nurse came to bring Dad up to the ward. Once we got there, a group of nurses started preparing him for surgery. The anaesthetist – a kind man wearing a large pounamu, which made us feel more at ease than he probably knew – came and explained his part in the procedure. The surgeon arrived shortly afterwards and did the same. He explained that the procedure was akin to an 'electrical tune-up'. Crystallising the surgery down to its raw mechanics was, for me, a helpful strategy. The surgeon was an autoelectrician in scrubs. Nothing more, nothing less.

Finally, it was time for the procedure. Two nurses came to collect Dad and take him through to the operating theatre. I kissed him on his forehead, as I always do, and gave him a hug for luck. He told me to go home and take care of Mum and my sister. He would call me once he was awake. Then the nurses removed the brakes on his bed and pushed it out of the room.

I remember watching him being wheeled down the hallway before taking a hard right down another corridor toward the operating room. I called after him, wishing him good luck. He lifted his arm and gave me a thumbs-up as the bed rounded the corner.

∽

By the early 2010s, the benefits of Keg's first ablation surgery had largely disappeared. His electrical wiring had found new ways to become discordant, and the trips to Middlemore Hospital had increased in frequency. By this time, I was living in Wellington, building a career in public health. I wasn't in Auckland to take him to the hospital or wish him luck before a procedure. The distance was hard, especially when he was unwell.

Dad's second ablation procedure happened when we were gearing up for a national study on the risk factors for rheumatic fever (more on that in later pages). His surgeon told him that he needed a little more electrical fine-tuning and that he was hopeful it might be the last one that he would need. The day of his procedure coincided with a significant work meeting for a separate project that I was involved in. I was presenting the preliminary findings for the project in front of our team, but could think of little else than my dad and that soldering iron. I gave perhaps the most distracted and disjointed presentation I've ever delivered.

Halfway through the results slides, my phone rang. It was my mum. Dad had made it through the procedure with flying colours. My heart sang. I returned to the meeting with a spring in my step and hit the remainder of the presentation out of the park.

The benefits of the second ablation procedure were longer-lasting than the first, but not indefinite. The soldering iron was not finished with Keg. A spectre hovered over his shoulder, guiding his health toward decline. We were all aware of it but rarely spoke of it, though, eventually, we would need to confront it head-on: Dad's leaky valve.

∽

Early valve surgeons were audacious and probably should not have attempted what they did with the technology of the early twentieth century. They did so anyway and crossed medical frontiers. Their audacity, however, pales in comparison to the courage of the first patients.

Most developments in valve repair or replacement have happened in the last 100 years. In 1925, a London surgeon named Henry Souttar treated a 15-year-old girl, whom Souttar named L.H. in his account, with severe valve dysfunction by cutting open her chest, sticking his finger into her left atrium and using it to render the valve flexible again.[6] The girl made a full recovery. However, the technique was panned by fellow surgeons as barbaric and unnecessary, and so it did not gain traction.[7]

Since 1925, technologies used to repair or replace damaged valves and surrounding tissue have developed quickly. The first mechanical valve was implanted in the early 1950s, saving patients with serious dysfunction of the valve between the aorta and ventricle.[8] The earliest versions of these valves were made of a ball of plastic the size of a small marble, which sat within a tube that was narrow at the ends and fat in the middle. With each heartbeat, the marble would move up and down the tube, opening and shutting the artificial valve.

These mechanical valves were prone to failure or rejection by the patient's body through the immune system's response to suspected foreign tissue. In the 1960s, surgeons pioneered the transplant of real valves from human donors into patients' hearts. Surgeon Donald Ross transplanted the first valve in 1962 at the National Heart Hospital in London. As Ross was operating, the donor valve disintegrated beneath his scalpel. He contacted a colleague at Oxford University, Alfred Gunning, who had been studying human valves in his laboratory. A frozen valve was rushed to the operating room, and Ross successfully sutured the first transplanted human heart valve into his patient.[9]

The problem with relying on human donor valves is that demand is always greater than supply. By the 1970s, the lack of human donor hearts was being relieved by animal hearts, such as those from pigs.[10] The limited lifespan of these valves meant that patients might need two or even three replacements. Also, the patient's immune system might reject the non-native valve.

As technology has advanced, so has the sophistication of the techniques that repair or replace valves. Mechanical valves, often made from titanium or carbon, as well as human and animal valves, are still used, but where once a surgeon pried the chest open and used a finger to open a valve, now they might thread a balloon up from the groin and inflate it to open a scarred or stuck valve. Where previously a surgeon might excise a faulty valve before replacing it, they might now sew a new one over the old one. This reduces the complexity of the procedure and risk to the patient.

I am relieved minimally invasive valve surgery is common practice now, since I am pretty sure my dad is going to require it before too long. Given how fast valve repair and replacement techniques have improved in recent decades, it seems the longer we delay a valve replacement, the better and safer the treatment options will be.

But waiting for better techniques and technology must be weighed against the damage that my father's leaky valve is doing to the shape and function of his heart. After his latest cardiac ablation surgery my father's surgeon told us his heart is significantly scarred from all the extra labour it has been doing over the last 50 years. So it is true that the longer we delay a new valve for Dad, the better. However, it's also true that a dead man has no use for one.

∽

While advancements in the treatment and management of rheumatic heart disease help patients live longer, ideally with improved quality of life, these advances don't address the disease's global burden. Like rates of rheumatic fever, cases of rheumatic heart disease have dropped precipitously over the past three decades. Between 1990 and 2015, the rate of global death from rheumatic heart disease fell by nearly 50 percent, from nine per 100,000 people to under five per 100,000.[11] If the mortality rate was the same in 2015 as it was in 1990, then we would have expected 320,000 more deaths from rheumatic heart disease in 2015 than were actually reported.

Rates of rheumatic heart disease and deaths resulting from it have fallen because they are tethered to the incidence of rheumatic fever. Without the latter, there is no former. As noted earlier, the dramatic drop in global rates of rheumatic fever has been largely attributed to improvements in living and working conditions in some combination with the prophylactic benefits of penicillin.[12] To be sure, these improvements have reduced exposure to *Group-A Strep* infection.

However, the global downturn masks the enduring and growing asymmetries between the populations that have rheumatic fever and rheumatic heart disease and those that do not. This creates the false impression that we are nearing global eradication of these diseases. The reality is different. Within developing countries, cases of both rheumatic fever and rheumatic heart disease remain far too high. Measuring the rate of progression from rheumatic fever to rheumatic heart disease is challenging because a lot of people diagnosed with rheumatic heart disease – 75 percent in a recent New Zealand study[13] – have no clinical record of a previous bout of rheumatic fever. But regardless of the true rate of progression, today in countries where rheumatic fever is rife, such as India, Pakistan and most Pacific islands, the prevalence of rheumatic heart disease is now approaching 450 cases per 100,000, compared to around three cases per 100,000 in Australia and New Zealand.[14] That those countries with the most cases of rheumatic heart disease are the least able to meet the ensuing health care demand is a cruel irony of modern medicine.

The prevalence of rheumatic heart disease is nearly 150 times higher within countries where rheumatic fever is common compared to those countries where it is not. If we couple this with the large and densely packed populations in countries where rheumatic heart disease is now common – such as India – we have reason to worry. For example, in 2015 there were more than 13 million cases of rheumatic heart disease in India alone.[15] But the starkest disparities are found *within* countries rather than between them. Right now, even after adjusting for differences in deprivation level, deaths from rheumatic heart disease are more than 10 times higher among Māori and Pacific peoples than among New Zealand Europeans.[16] In Australia, more than eight of every 10 new cases of rheumatic heart disease are diagnosed among Indigenous Australians, and seven of every 10 rheumatic heart disease deaths happen among this population.[17] In New Zealand and Australia, it appears that rheumatic fever and rheumatic heart disease are well on the way to being eliminated for everyone – except Indigenous and Pacific peoples.

Māori and Pacific patients with rheumatic heart disease die on average at age 60, while non-Māori and non-Pacific patients with the same disease die at around age 80.[18] These are more than mere statistics; my father is embedded in those numbers. The Māori boy from Northland who was 30 times more likely to develop rheumatic fever than his New Zealand European schoolmates is also much less likely to survive into old age than a New Zealand European with the same disease.

These disparities ought to make us uncomfortable. Though things may seem to be getting better, a substantial minority is still underserved. Why do these disparities persist? Why, when many countries have been able to largely eliminate rheumatic fever, are so many people still suffering?

Chapter Six
The causes of rheumatic fever

IN 2013, a group led by infectious disease epidemiologist and University of Otago professor Michael Baker embarked on a quest to figure out exactly what was causing rheumatic fever, and why – despite the overall low rates of the disease – particular communities remained so at risk. Baker's team brought together epidemiologists, paediatricians, cardiologists, immunologists and microbiologists. The goal was ambitious: to pinpoint the disease's causes once and for all. The country's shame would become science's gain.

Previous studies had fundamental weaknesses that prevented researchers from gaining an accurate appreciation of the most important causes of rheumatic fever. Some studies simply did not have enough cases of the disease from which to draw meaningful conclusions. Some, like the ones conducted at US Army camps in the early 1940s, drew conclusions through mere observation, recording, for example, how many soldiers slept in a barracks and comparing that to how many cases of rheumatic fever occurred there. It was a good start, but the evidence was largely circumstantial.

The research team's first step was to conduct a nationwide study of children suffering from rheumatic fever in New Zealand. The team would attempt to recruit all the cases of rheumatic fever that occurred in New Zealand over several years, and they would do it in real time – as soon as children were diagnosed. For the second step, the study team would then recruit two or three 'controls' for every rheumatic fever case. The controls were matched to the rheumatic fever 'cases' by such factors as age, sex, location and ethnicity. Then, the study would compare a wide range of results between the two groups: blood tests, throat and nose swabs, genetic tests, hair samples and detailed information about the child's environment. The latter was determined from the study's comprehensive questionnaire, which would enquire about everything from the number of sore throat episodes children had to how many sugary drinks they normally consumed daily.

The team's apparently simple goal of defining the causes of rheumatic fever was quickly eclipsed by the complexity of the task. Geography was one initial problem. Professor Baker's team was based in Wellington. While plenty of rheumatic fever cases could be found in the outskirts of the city in areas such as Porirua and Wainuiomata, these numbers paled in comparison to the volume found several hundred kilometres north in Auckland and Northland. Of all the rheumatic fever cases diagnosed in New Zealand in a given year, the majority will occur in these two regions.

Timing was another obstacle. Typically, a three-week lag separates a child's hospitalisation with a diagnosis of rheumatic fever from the sore throat or skin infection that initiated the immune response leading to the disease.[1] This delay meant the team needed to recruit the ill children as soon as possible after they were diagnosed. This was partly to minimise the chance of patients and families forgetting what they had been doing just before diagnosis and partly to ensure the *Group-A Strep* in the throat swab were still alive by the time a swab was taken. This 'need for speed' usually meant collecting data from children still in acute care wards. It involved considerable cooperation from the clinicians treating the patients, as well as from the children themselves and their families. Collection of the data was a time-consuming and often intrusive process, happening at a time when families were at their most vulnerable. Once permission was granted, it could take over an hour to draw blood, collect the swabs, clip hair and gather answers to wide-ranging questions about such things as family history, diet and living conditions.

The question of who would grant permission on behalf of the child for these and other interventions could also be complicated. The average age of patients diagnosed with rheumatic fever in New Zealand is around nine years old, and more than 80 percent of all cases are aged between five and 19.[2] The research team needed to consult carefully with families to confirm who had the power to consent, on the child's behalf, to participation in this intensive study. Sometimes one parent or guardian agreed, but another did not.

Culture was another factor to consider. Nearly all cases of rheumatic fever in New Zealand are among Māori (more than 50 percent) or Pacific peoples (nearly 40 percent). As such, despite making up around 25 percent of the New Zealand population, these two groups represent around 90 percent of the cases of rheumatic fever.[3] Research in which a predominantly European research team studies a predominantly non-European population carries a risk of 'othering', a reductive action where researchers do all the talking for the 'subject' group, despite having no authority to do so. To avoid this risk, the research team needed strong partnerships with Māori and Pacific researchers, clinicians and community members.

These were not the only factors the research team needed to consider in late 2013. How were they going to match cases to controls and ensure that the comparisons were accurate? How would running a study with vulnerable children be balanced against the need to ensure this once-in-a-generation study captured every significant aspect of those children's lives? How would a blood sample collected at a hospital at the top of the North Island be preserved so it was still viable upon arrival for analysis at a South Island laboratory?

Recognising the magnitude of his study, Professor Baker assembled as many people in New Zealand working in the field of rheumatic fever as possible. The study didn't need just infectious disease experts, data collectors and lab technicians to be a success. It also required frontline clinical staff in each region to ensure it could quickly approach rheumatic fever cases soon after diagnosis.

In 2013, my position as a research fellow at the University of Otago Medical School in Wellington was coming to an end. I was looking for a new job, ideally in epidemiology, to support myself and my small family. That same year, the Health Research Council, New Zealand's major health research funding organisation, had requested research proposals in the area of rheumatic fever. Money had been gathered from a number of sources, including the Ministry of Health, Te Puni Kōkiri (the Ministry of Māori Development), the New Zealand Heart Foundation, Cure Kids (a child-focused charity) and the Health Research Council itself. Around NZ$3 million was to be invested in the research.

When Professor Baker reached out to those who might be interested in joining his team, I jumped at the chance. Keg had a cardioversion earlier that year, and was preparing for his second cardiac ablation. Here was an opportunity to mix practical responsibility with personal satisfaction. I would be able to support my family financially while also fighting rheumatic fever – fighting for Keg, my family and myself. With the research project approved, I was very happy to find myself managing the most comprehensive study ever undertaken on the causes of rheumatic fever. The study was called the Rheumatic Fever Risk Factors study, or RF RISK.

To be effective, the study would need a large number of participants. Ensuring that we could recruit as many participants into the study as possible required us to get strong buy-in from the clinical staff charged with their care. While all agreed that the disease was serious and intolerably unfair in who it attacked, the study still had its sceptics: some believed that we already knew enough to take large-scale public health action against the causes of rheumatic fever, and others doubted our ability to take this action even if we had all the answers. We needed a public relations roadshow of sorts, so (now-deceased) paediatrician Professor Dinny Lennon and I went on tour. We visited hospitals and medical practices throughout the country, meeting with clinicians and their teams, transforming some of them from study sceptics into devoted champions. In this way, we built a cohesive national network of clinical collaborators within the study team and beyond. These efforts ensured that the first time a patient and their family heard about the study, it would be from a supporter of the research. With our clinical champions on board, we could rapidly detect and recruit rheumatic fever cases from around the country, even from small regional hospitals.

Achieving sufficient cultural competence and safety within the study was vital. We needed Māori and Pacific governance. We established two panels, composed respectively of Māori and Pacific researchers, clinicians and community workers. As study manager and one of the Māori members of the wider team, I took on the role of leading the Māori panel. We called these 'steering groups', not 'advisory' panels, because the former denoted real decision-making power. To make this clear, we determined that all data and specimens collected during the study would be 'guarded' by these groups and that any use to which they might be put would first require their approval.

At our first meeting after funding for the RF RISK study had been secured in 2013, the research team debated the scope of the project. Would we use this opportunity to collect data on the widest possible range of risk factors, everything from genetic predisposition to poor oral health? Or should we use our resources to hone in on factors currently considered to pose the greatest risk, like housing quality and overcrowding?

I believed strongly that we should collect as much data as possible. This belief came partly from my original training in biomechanics at the University of Auckland with Professor Uwe Kersting, who had taught me to make the most of the time a patient gives by collecting as much information as possible. I also saw this study as a once-in-a-generation opportunity to learn about the formation of this disease. What if my father's poor oral health, driven by a fear of the 'murder house', as children used to refer to school dental clinics, was the catalyst for his rheumatic fever?[4] Or maybe his daily fruit consumption was relevant, or whether he was breastfed as a baby? I wanted to know every detail, no matter how insignificant it seemed.

Eventually everyone agreed that the study should aim to identify as many potential risk factors as possible. To do anything less, we decided, would be a disservice to the children and families who would be giving their time and precious energy to participate in the study, as well as to future generations.

The RF RISK study got underway in early 2014, at first only in Auckland and Northland. Before long, we were operating in every region around the country where rheumatic fever was endemic. By the end of 2017, we had collected sufficient data and closed recruitment. It would take another two years to fully complete the analysis for the project, and the challenges posed by the COVID-19 pandemic further delayed formal publication of the results. The work was often arduous, but nearly all the challenges of the project were overcome with excellent teamwork. By 2022, we had completed and published a world-class study and contributed significantly to understanding the main causes of rheumatic fever.

∽

A *Group-A Strep* infection is a necessary link in the chain that leads to rheumatic fever, but it isn't the only link. If it were, everyone who got strep throat would always get rheumatic fever, which is not the case. Most *Group-A Strep* infections are cured without the bacteria ever breaking free from its original landing zone at the back of our throats or on our skin. There are other factors – perhaps genetic or environmental, perhaps both – that make a child more or less susceptible to rheumatic fever once they've been infected with *Group-A Strep*.

Ideally, we would be able to stop a *Group-A Strep* infection from occurring in the first place: no *Group-A Strep* infection, no rheumatic fever. A similar idea was behind an attempt to reduce rates of the disease in New Zealand, the Rheumatic Fever Prevention Programme (RFPP). This $65 million venture was established in 2011 by the New Zealand Government with the aim of reducing the incidence of rheumatic fever by two thirds within five years.[5] It was an ambitious goal, made more so by the absence of a clear path to achieving it. Lacking clear, New Zealand-specific evidence about what causes rheumatic fever – such as the RF RISK study aimed to gather – the programme had to progress on hunches and best guesses. Those working in rheumatic fever prevention or care embraced the goal while simultaneously questioning its viability.

A major intervention arising from the educated guesses made by the RFPP was an expansive – and expensive – school-based throat-swabbing programme. The underlying premise was simple: if *Group-A Strep* infections lead to rheumatic fever, then catching

Group-A Strep infections early and treating them quickly might cut cases of *Group-A Strep*-related illness and, in turn, rheumatic fever. The premise had been tested in New Zealand in the late 1990s among 22,000 children across 53 schools, of which half had access to a school-based sore throat clinic programme and half did not. The results of the large trial had been underwhelming, with only a marginal drop in rheumatic fever among those who had access to the sore throat clinics.[6] Yet the idea of a national school-based throat swabbing programme did have support from several leading academics and clinicians working in childhood infectious diseases, and was enthusiastically supported by coalface health workers and community advocates. Finally, after decades of neglect, here was some widespread and visible action at the community level.

In 2011, armed with a clear message and goal, community workers, advocates, teachers and nurses went to work. The sore throat programme was implemented in 10 District Health Board regions around New Zealand, embedding throat swabbing programmes into primary and intermediate schools. At the same time, an extensive advertising campaign was underway to raise awareness of the connection between sore throats and rheumatic fever, with television and print media showing images of children with large scars on their chests following open-heart surgery for rheumatic heart disease. Most of the RFPP's $65 million, however, was invested in the school throat swabbing programme.

Four years after it had been established, in 2015, the Ministry of Health commissioned an evaluation of the school-based component of the programme. As with the trial from the late 1990s, results from regions offering the sore throat clinics showed there was no significant reduction in rheumatic fever risk for children who received the school programme compared with those who did not.[7] Cases of rheumatic fever did decline midway through the programme, but the downturn was short-lived, and rates rapidly returned to pre-programme levels.

The results from the RFPP highlight the central issue that faced our RF RISK research team: stomping out rheumatic fever was a more complex undertaking than a throat swabbing programme could solve. We needed to dig deeper and learn more about what was driving the disease to affect some but not others.

By the end of the RF RISK study, we had a trove of data with which to formulate some insights into the causes of rheumatic fever. We had certainly caught some interesting fish by casting our net wide. However, with the many intersecting and overlapping risk factors, it was difficult to know where to start. To make sense of the data, we broke these factors down into conceptual groups. First, we focused on those factors related to the bacteria; second, we focused on factors related to people (or 'the host'); and third, we looked at the environments in which people lived.

The bacteria

We know that there are over 200 unique kinds of *Group-A Strep*.[8] After being infected, a person may only develop immunity to the specific strain that caused the infection. This is why the effectiveness of the various vaccines against COVID-19 has waned, as new variants of the coronavirus that cause the disease have evolved. It was previously thought that some strains of *Group-A Strep* might be more likely to lead to rheumatic fever than others, but this idea is currently debunked.[9] An infection with one strain of *Group-A Strep* doesn't necessarily mean you're immune from a different one, and many, if not all, strains can lead to rheumatic fever. This makes developing an effective vaccine against rheumatic fever extremely challenging.

A *Group-A Strep* vaccine does not yet exist. If we could vaccinate against *Group-A Strep*, we would remove the trigger before the immune system has a chance to pull it. Moreover, if a broad-spectrum vaccine were developed, one that covered all strains of *Group-A Strep* that lead to an auto-aggressive response from our immune system, then the recipient would not only be immune to rheumatic fever but also to the other conditions that *Group-A Strep* causes; such as the glomerulonephritis that killed Mozart or the streptococcal toxic shock syndrome that killed Jim Henson.

Vaccination against *Group-A Strep*, which is responsible for more than half a million deaths per year worldwide, is an appealing prospect.[10] The World Health Organization has made developing a *Group-A Strep* vaccine an international priority. In the last few years, New Zealand and Australia have invested heavily in research to accelerate the vaccine's development.[11]

In New Zealand, we vaccinate our population against roughly 20 diseases, with COVID-19 being the latest to join the list. Although the mechanisms vary from vaccine to vaccine, they basically follow the same principle Edward Jenner identified in the 1790s when he cut the skin of an eight-year-old boy and put cowpox cells on the wound (simultaneously ushering in both the solution to smallpox and the concept of vaccination). We introduce trace elements (real or synthetic) of a disease-causing virus or bacteria, stimulating the immune system to respond.[12] The immune system then stores information in our memory cells, so that if the virus or bacteria reappears, it can eliminate the infection before it becomes serious.

While researching for this book, I returned to my former campus at the University of Auckland Medical School. I wanted to speak to my friend and colleague, Associate Professor Nikki Moreland, who specialises in the immunological response to rheumatic fever. Nikki also happens to be one of New Zealand's eminent minds when it comes to developing a *Group-A Strep* vaccine. As such, she was well-placed to inform me about when a vaccine might appear.

Nikki explained that creating a vaccine faces a significant obstacle since we still don't know exactly how the immune system causes rheumatic fever. 'It won't be easy,' she continued, 'given that extra hurdle and the sheer number of *Group-A Strep* strain types, but there are some really promising vaccines in the early stages of development.' These promising early signs and the recent funding support from governments and international consortia mean we now have growing momentum in the search.

'It feels like a pivotal time for *Group-A Strep* vaccines. So yes, I think there's hope,' Nikki said.

The hunt for a vaccine may look hopeful, but even if one is found, it will not solve the underlying drivers of *Group-A Strep* infection. The elimination of rheumatic fever from most developed countries did not occur because of a vaccine but was due to improvements in living conditions. To be most effective, vaccination needs to happen alongside the substantial social reform that it will take to address the social determinants of rheumatic fever.

∽

The vast number of *Group-A Strep* strains doesn't just have implications for vaccine development. It also makes it harder to mount an effective public health response to outbreaks. If only a few strains of *Group-A Strep* caused rheumatic fever, community surveillance programmes could be set up to search for these and provide treatment and preventative regimes if these strains were found. However, *Group-A Strep* is everywhere, and any strain might cause rheumatic fever at any time. A further conundrum is that while *Group-A Strep* infection is very common, subsequent rheumatic fever is relatively rare. For every 100,000 (mostly) children in Auckland whose throat swabs test positive for *Group-A Strep*, around 40 go on to develop rheumatic fever within three months.[13] For every 100,000 skin swabs, the number that progress to rheumatic fever in three months is only 20. This leads to the question of why some people progress from a *Group-A Strep* infection to rheumatic fever and some do not.

The host

The RF RISK study confirmed that some factors make a person more susceptible to rheumatic fever. The first is age since, almost exclusively, the disease affects children. But not just any children. Rheumatic fever is extremely rare among those under five years of age. Over the course of our multi-year RF RISK study, I could count the number of rheumatic fever cases among children under five in New Zealand on my fingers.[14] This unusual phenomenon may provide a critical clue in determining what makes a host susceptible to rheumatic fever: as alluded to earlier, current thinking suggests that for a *Group-A Strep* infection to progress to rheumatic fever, the host needs to have a blossoming immune system,[15] one that has seen some action but remains relatively innocent.

We also need to consider the host's ethnicity. Since almost all cases of the disease happen among only a handful of ethnic groups, it would be easy to conclude that some inherent genetic factor makes Māori and Pacific peoples in New Zealand and Aboriginal and Torres Strait Islanders in Australia, among others, more susceptible to the disease. In the RF RISK study, we found that if all of a child's grandparents were either Māori or Pacific, their risk of rheumatic fever jumped by more than five times compared to those with at least one non-Māori or non-Pacific grandparent.

On the face of it, this finding suggests a genetic predisposition to inherited risk. However, the genetic theory is weak since, as we have seen, up until the last 50 years or so, rheumatic fever was internationally an overwhelmingly European condition until living conditions in countries with large European populations improved. RF RISK study data suggest it's more likely that the relationship between ethnicity and rheumatic fever has to do with the social differences between ethnic groups and their exposure to the environments that foster the proliferation of *Group-A Strep*. As Māori political leader Dame Tariana Turia noted in a speech on rheumatic fever in 2014: 'We are not born to be vulnerable.'[16]

A family history of rheumatic fever certainly adds to a child's risk of getting the disease. Here, the evidence is unequivocal. The RF RISK study, along with others,[17] found that if a child had a blood relative who had previously had rheumatic fever, their risk of developing the disease increased by nearly five times. However, the reasons for this added susceptibility are uncertain. As mentioned earlier, there is scant evidence that a shared genetic aberration might play a part. As with the increased risk of having Māori or Pacific ancestry, the most plausible current theory is that rheumatic fever's recurrence among blood relatives reflects the fact that families share similar physical and social environments.

'Environment' encompasses where a person lives, the resources they have access to and their social status. Whether a family is well educated or not influences their level of knowledge about health (health literacy), which in turn can influence whether or not a parent seeks immediate medical care when a child complains of a sore throat. Even accounting for levels of health literacy, the RF RISK study found that patients with rheumatic fever were twice as likely to face barriers to timely care as those who didn't develop rheumatic fever.

The RF RISK team examined the relationship between hosts and rheumatic fever and concluded that susceptible hosts may only be as susceptible as the environment in which they were born and live.

The environment

The environment we live in shapes our health. If fast food restaurants and liquor stores populate our childhood neighbourhood, we're more likely to become obese and have a drinking problem than if we live in a neighbourhood with gyms and health food stores.[18] The same cause and effect applies to rheumatic fever. If we grow up in environments where *Group-A Strep* can easily breed and spread, our chances of developing rheumatic fever increase.

Since the early studies of streptococcal outbreaks in World War II army barracks, observers have strongly suspected that rheumatic fever development is related to crowding. The RF RISK study proved the relationship between household crowding and the risk of rheumatic fever.[19] *Group-A Strep* spreads best when people are grouped closely together, especially indoors. (The COVID-19 pandemic was a reminder of this, albeit with viral, not bacterial, contagion.) Children who lived in severely crowded homes were almost four times more likely to develop rheumatic fever than those who did not, even after accounting for other influential factors, such as how cold or damp the house was. An overcrowded house may not necessarily have too many people in too few rooms. There may be plenty of space, but a large family may choose to sleep in one or two rooms. During the RF RISK study, interviewers heard a common story from families of children who had developed rheumatic fever: in winter, they crammed the children into the only room with a reliable heat source.

Overcrowding leads to other risky practices in the context of rheumatic fever. For example, one family member may share a bed with another, and this close proximity will increase the night-time transfer of *Group-A Strep*, as likely happened to Keg during his tournament in 1969. In the RF RISK study, we found that sharing a bed increased the risk of a child developing rheumatic fever compared to those who didn't share a bed, even after accounting for other factors, such as how crowded the house was.

The structural health of a house also matters. New Zealand homes may make children sick. The age of a house, how damp it is, and how much mould grows around windows and down curtains – all of these have been found by the RF RISK study in New Zealand and similar studies around the world to increase the chance of *Group-A Strep* infection and rheumatic fever.[20]

A wider issue is housing tenure: whether one owns or rents a dwelling. The quality of a house is generally poorer if it is a rental. Previous research shows the risk of rheumatic fever directly correlates to whether a family owns or rents their home.[21] In the RF RISK study, renting a home, as opposed to owning one, increased the risk of rheumatic fever more than threefold, even after accounting for such factors as socioeconomic deprivation. This makes homeownership a public health concern.

A child's home environment can increase their risk of rheumatic fever in unexpected ways. One is so basic it might embarrass developed countries such as New Zealand: access to hot water. We found that a lack of hot water for bathing more than doubled the risk of a child developing rheumatic fever. This may be because hot water reduces the amount of *Group-A Strep* that can live on a child's skin. However, hot water probably represents something more significant. When we accounted for other housing factors, such as crowding and dampness, the link between hot water and rheumatic fever weakened. Hot water may just indicate whether a family has secure access to the essential resources that ensure a healthy standard of living inside their child's home.

Access to a clean, healthy environment does protect against skin infections, and evidence continues to grow regarding skin sores as a potential entry point for *Group-A Strep*. In the RF RISK study, we found that children who recently had a skin infection were more than twice as likely to develop rheumatic fever compared to those who had not. The study of nearly two million swabs taken from throats and skin throughout the Auckland region found that a *Group-A Strep-*

positive skin swab was indeed linked to rheumatic fever, although not as strongly as a positive throat swab. This link was most profound among Māori and Pacific peoples.[22] These other studies support our finding that skin infection is probably an important part of the rheumatic fever story.[23]

These key findings from RF RISK and other studies have led to a paradigm shift in our understanding of how and why children still develop rheumatic fever in New Zealand. The recent evidence paints a troubling picture. It exposes the uncomfortable truth that cases of rheumatic fever within developed countries are deeply rooted in social injustice and inequity. It increasingly looks as though the elimination of rheumatic fever will only be achieved by addressing the crucial issue of how social forces affect health.

Chapter Seven
The causes of the causes I: Poor housing

IMAGINE you are standing outside a front door. The door is the main entrance to whatever you imagine a typical house in a high-deprivation area looks like. It is a cold, wet, windy day. There is a large gap in the seal between the door and the surrounding joinery. The wind is pushing through the gap, creating a whistling noise.

You open the door and are immediately hit by a strong, dank smell. The air feels too thick to breathe because of the moisture. The carpets are old and tattered, and the walls and ceiling are wafer-thin. The temperature *inside* the house is nearly identical to the temperature *outside*, if not somehow colder.

You walk down a dark, musty hallway into a small children's bedroom. You see that there are two children's names in bright pink lettering on the door, but when you walk into the room, only a single bed sits against one of the walls. The room is mostly dark, with little natural light. You notice black specks of mould climbing up the wall behind the bed, congregating in corners and edges. There is a window on the wall adjacent to the bed and a small desk for doing homework beneath it. The wooden joinery around the window is ancient; the single-glazed panes equally so. The window is closed to capture the small amount of heat inside the room. Moisture teems down the inside of the closed window as if it is raining both outside and inside.

It is so cold and damp in the bedroom that you have started to shiver, so you walk back into the hallway on the hunt for a source of heat. You walk into the small kitchen and notice a colourful hand-drawn chart on the fridge: upon closer inspection, you see that it is a hot shower roster for the week. You continue to move from room to room, searching for heat, to no avail – until you notice a small oil heater in the centre of the family room. You see several sleeping bags on the floor next to the heater, surrounded by comics and colouring-in books. There is less mould here, but the air is just as thick and damp. Here, too, the windows are crying.

The above scenario probably seems intentionally bleak. However, each specific detail – the bed-sharing, the damp air, the mould, the heater – is based on direct evidence from the RF RISK study. This scenario isn't hypothetical but rather a dramatisation of real-world data. It illustrates that, in all important respects, rheumatic fever begins at home.

∞

Middlemore Hospital in South Auckland serves a large Māori and Pacific population. Located in one of the poorest regions in New Zealand, the hospital's paediatric ward deals with most of Auckland's poverty-related childhood illnesses. The RF RISK team knew that confirming their commitment to the study would be crucial to gathering sufficient data to form meaningful conclusions. Although we planned to operate around the country, we expected about half our patients to be recruited through Middlemore Hospital. It was, therefore, essential that we secure the support of their paediatric team.

Throughout 2013 I travelled with paediatrician Professor Dinny Lennon, visiting clinical teams throughout New Zealand on our clinical roadshow. We would explain that our research aimed to identify the root causes of rheumatic fever, outline our plans for the study and ask if they would help us recruit newly diagnosed patients from their hospitals. Visits were always easier when Professor Lennon was in the room. Her decades of experience as a rheumatic fever champion preceded her, and she knew everyone around the country working in rheumatic fever prevention and care. For our Middlemore Hospital visit, Professor Lennon and I met with her colleagues in a windowless room. We didn't need to work to sell the idea of the study. These clinicians were all too familiar with the signs and symptoms of rheumatic fever in the children they looked after. They instantly recognised that this was a real opportunity to learn how to prevent rheumatic fever and stop the steady flow of children being admitted to their wards with throbbing joints and swollen hearts. It also helped that Middlemore was where Professor Lennon did much of her clinical work, so she was a close colleague of most of the team. Eventually, our conversation turned from the details of the study to the difficulties they often experienced in the clinical management of rheumatic fever.

One staff member drew attention to the crippling shortage of ultrasound technicians in the Auckland region, which meant that the waiting list for heart scans for children recovering from rheumatic fever could stretch to months. To make matters worse, technicians were resigning from their public sector jobs in favour of the higher salaries offered in private practice. Families unable to afford access to private ultrasounds had no choice but to join the ever-lengthening backlog on the public waiting list. The dangerous delays in appointments would persist until there is an increase in the number of ultrasound technicians in public hospitals. Our talk moved from problems accessing heart scans to other difficulties with post-diagnostic care. Children with rheumatic fever need long-term intensive treatment and follow-up. Because getting rheumatic fever again can worsen any heart problems caused by the first episode, it's essential that they go onto a sustained, long-term course of prophylactic antibiotics. This currently involves receiving a painful injection of penicillin directly into a big muscle, such as the thigh or buttock, every month until at least the age of 21 – older if there are any signs of rheumatic heart disease. Adherence to this demanding regimen is an enormous challenge, one of the battlefronts where repeated encounters with rheumatic fever are either won or lost. Some programmes have nurses visit distant communities to administer antibiotics, but these programmes are often at risk of having their funding cut.

We also discussed a brand-new programme getting underway at the time, called AWHI, or Auckland Wide Housing Initiative (it's a nice coincidence that 'awhi' also means 'hug' in te reo Māori). AWHI was part of a broader government programme called the Healthy Homes Initiative. Under this programme, teams were set up to support any child discharged from Middlemore Hospital who had been diagnosed with a poverty-related illness. Situations that triggered an AWHI response included households with children at high risk of rheumatic fever (such as a child hospitalised with rheumatic fever symptoms), a member of a household with a past episode of rheumatic fever, or multiple *Group-A Strep* infections within a household over a three-month period.[1] The criteria also included evidence of structural or functional crowding within a household, and evidence of socioeconomic deprivation. The support team looked at the family's housing and organised whatever interventions were necessary to improve it to a healthy standard. The goal was to ensure that unwell children returned to a warm, dry home. If, for example, a house lacked curtains, heating, good bedding, carpets or ventilation, AWHI would provide these.

At first, this programme appeared to be a cause for optimism and relief. It represented a direct intervention to improve health through housing quality. Here, at last, was a programme that was unafraid to directly confront the social determinants of rheumatic fever by lifting the standard of living for those at risk of poverty-related illnesses. To ensure the people of South Auckland were served, Māori health providers working within their own communities ran AWHI. I was delighted.

However, after explaining the programme's virtues, the team mapped out some of the obstacles to its success. Some families that would have benefitted from the programme had missed out because, even though they lived in dire conditions, they weren't poor enough in terms of income to qualify. Moreover, even if family members qualified, referring them into the programme meant convincing them that their home might be making their child severely ill. This well-meaning approach risked creating profound personal shame among parents and caregivers. These negotiations happened alongside longstanding mistrust between the government and colonised or otherwise marginalised populations. After generations of condescension and abuse, it should come as no surprise that some families would resist the idea of letting the government snoop around their homes.

The major obstacle, though, was resourcing. 'The problem,' one of the staff said, 'is that the demand is too great. It all sounds good on paper, but in reality we don't have the resources that are needed to fix such a big problem.'

Here was a service that, to my mind, represented the most important step yet in reducing South Auckland's burden of rheumatic fever. But from the perspective of those who referred families, the programme was ineffective because it could not keep up with the demand it had helped to expose. The Middlemore Hospital clinicians were optimistic about the programme's future and believed strongly in the value of a community-based solution to a problem that was usually dealt with in the emergency room. They were also optimistic that, in time, decision-makers would recognise the programme's virtues, and substantial and sustainable funding would follow. But for the time being, the support teams of paediatricians, nurses and care coordinators were caught between wanting the best post-discharge outcomes for their patients and wanting to avoid giving false hope to vulnerable families.

∞

The house that Keg grew up in still sits on the main road that stretches away from Whangārei city, past the hospital and cemetery, and out into the countryside. I drive past it every time I visit the graves of family and friends buried in the cemetery. If my wife and children are in the car, I will often point out Keg's house to them as we drive by.

The single-storey, three-bedroomed weatherboard house is cream with a maroon-red roof. At a modest 100 square metres, it looks very small compared to the large section that surrounds it. It would have been a home that a working-class family could be immensely proud of when it was built in the 1920s. Time has been somewhat unkind, and the road is now a state highway, but Keg's childhood home is by no means derelict.

Keg's family weren't particularly poor, nor were they well-off. With two parents, five children, and one income, the money had to stretch. They owned the local fish and chip shop, meaning that dinner time often involved leftover fish. Keg has strong memories of eating bits of the animal that really shouldn't be eaten and of months of smoked mullet, cooked in every possible variation by his mum.

Keg doesn't specifically remember the house being crowded, although with seven bodies it was often busy. Like many teenage boys, he spent most of his time outside the house rather than in it. He loved rugby more than anything, and his club – Hora Hora RFC – was just down the road. He remembers walking to school on cold winter mornings and standing in cow pats to warm his feet. Whether the latter is an apocryphal tale is something that he'll probably take to his grave.

It's hard to know for sure how the house that Keg grew up in influenced his development of rheumatic fever. Perhaps the house was bitterly cold, which is why he has such strong memories of cold winters despite living in the temperate north of New Zealand. Perhaps the close living environment within the modest home meant that he encountered repeat *Group-A Strep* infection as he grew up, which primed his immune system to respond the way it did after the winter tournament in 1969. We can only say with some certainty that these conditions probably increased Keg's propensity for *Group-A Strep* infection and subsequent rheumatic fever. Accordingly, we can also say with some certainty that improving those conditions would have reduced that propensity.

∽

The link between poor housing and poor health has been well established in research studies worldwide. Sub-standard housing – that is, housing that falls below certain internationally accepted health and safety standards – contributes to significantly higher rates of respiratory and cardiovascular disease, as well as the transmission of infectious diseases.[2] With their developing immune systems, children bear a disproportionate burden of housing-related illness: in New Zealand, around 18,000 children are admitted to hospital every year with conditions that might have been prevented through better quality housing.[3] By 'better' quality, I mean housing that, at the very least, is warm and dry. Unfortunately, New Zealand is a country where a lot of the housing stock is 'old, cold, and full of mould'.[4]

The World Health Organisation's recommended temperature for maintaining a healthy home is 18°C, increased to 20°C for families with small children.[5] The average indoor air temperature of a typical Kiwi home is 16°C.[6] Dampness from leaks and inadequate ventilation adds to the problem of cold. If the air inside a home is damp, it's much harder to heat than if the air is dry. It's best to first remove moisture from the air with a dehumidifier and then turn on the heater. Damp conditions promote the growth of mould on surfaces like walls, ceilings and carpets. The colder and mouldier their house, the greater the chance a child has of getting sick.[7]

Gold-star standard, warm, dry homes are distributed unequally among New Zealand's population. Statistically, Māori and Pacific peoples are less likely to occupy these more healthy homes and more likely to live in the kinds of damp, cold conditions that foster ill health. Accordingly, Māori and Pacific children are much more likely than other ethnic groups in New Zealand to suffer childhood illnesses because of poor housing stock.[8]

The RF RISK study clearly showed that poorly built housing puts children at risk of rheumatic fever. Two thirds of the children with rheumatic fever in the study lived in cold, damp and mouldy houses. These home environments seem to act like giant Petri dishes. One likely reason for this is that low indoor temperatures can change the way a family lives in their home. Since damp air is hard to heat and most New Zealand houses lack central heating, families tend to crowd together when the weather turns cold. Like the room with the oil heater in our thought experiment, everybody might congregate in one warm room before retiring to drafty bedrooms. Or, if it is too cold in the bedrooms, a family might sleep together in that one warm room. Our study confirmed what the US Army studies of the 1940s had observed: overcrowding leads to the spread of bacteria such as *Group-A Strep*. This, in turn, increases the risk of rheumatic fever.

Homeownership relates to housing quality and directly affects health. The RF RISK study showed that of every 10 children who developed rheumatic fever, around eight lived in a rental home.[9] Renting, it seems, is not good for your health: a 2018 New Zealand survey showed that owning a home is best, followed by living in a government-owned home. Houses on the private rental market are the unhealthiest.[10] Occupants of rental accommodation lack control over structural aspects of their living environment and must hope for a reliable landlord to improve substandard living conditions. Given New Zealand's persistent housing crisis, in which demand outstrips supply in many communities, landlords have little reason to prioritise spending money on improvements, and a renter, grateful to have a place to live, may be very reluctant to complain.

The fact that rental homes are less healthy than owner-occupied houses is significant for the two ethnic New Zealand populations that are so disproportionately over-represented in the country's rheumatic fever rates. In the late 1980s, around 50 percent of Māori and Pacific peoples lived in owner-occupied housing. By the mid-2010s, this was down to around 40 percent for Māori and 33 percent for Pacific peoples.[11] That means that around 60 to 70 percent of Māori and Pacific New Zealanders live in rental housing. Māori and Pacific peoples are more likely to live in poor-quality homes, the kind of housing that should have been brought up to a healthy standard or torn down and replaced decades ago.

Housing, then, is a potent determinant of health in general and the development of rheumatic fever specifically. The elimination of rheumatic fever from most of the developed world can be credited to improvements in living conditions, including a reduction in crowding. Yet the disease has endured in New Zealand and other pockets of the world, perhaps exactly because we have not paid enough attention to the environments in which we live. A substantial minority remain at increased risk of rheumatic fever and other housing-related diseases because the available housing stock is simply not fit for purpose – and because, for the most part, those who are most deeply affected have lacked the resources, social capital and political power to do anything about it.

∽

Improving New Zealand's housing stock is not going to happen quickly. Building regulations now set minimum insulation standards for new constructions. However, this does not tend to help the families whose children are being diagnosed with rheumatic fever. The majority of new dwellings are either owner-occupied or added to the high-end private rental market.

There are more promising programmes in place. The New Zealand government's Healthy Homes Initiative, which started in Auckland in 2013 with the AWHI programme, now operates throughout the country. It aims to increase the number of families who are housed in warm, dry accommodation and, in doing so, reduce the frequency and severity of illness for those living in those homes. A specific goal of the initiative is to upgrade the living conditions of families whose children are considered at greatest risk of rheumatic fever, either by improving their existing housing or by putting them on a 'Rheumatic Fever Fast Track' to new state houses. The programme also targets other housing- and poverty-related diseases, such as meningitis and asthma, and provides practical home improvement support ranging from curtains to ventilation and insulation.

The Healthy Homes Initiative has helped to expose the extent of the housing problem in New Zealand. Between 2015 and 2018, the Wellington arm of the initiative, known as 'Well Homes', carried out 900 initial house assessments. Nearly half of the dwellings checked needed additional insulation or were completely uninsulated, and so needed a total renovation.[12] Of the homes assessed, nine in 10 were mouldy, and eight in 10 had insufficient heating. The Healthy Homes Initiative has not only uncovered the need for better housing but also that it is possible to take widespread action to change the living conditions of our most vulnerable peoples.

Another New Zealand housing improvement initiative is the Warmer Kiwi Homes programme (formerly Warm Up New Zealand). Since 2009, this programme has subsidised home insulation, with an emphasis on persons or families with low incomes. This is the largest national housing improvement programme in New Zealand's history. By 2017, the New Zealand government had invested nearly half a billion dollars in insulation retrofits throughout New Zealand.[13] In 2018, the government announced an additional $140 million to further improve insulation in low-income households.[14] The Warmer Kiwi Homes programme has its shortcomings. For instance, it provides funding without much follow-up. It lacks the dexterity and community vision of AWHI, Well Homes and other programmes integrated under the Healthy Homes Initiative, which require people from affected local communities, from public servants and academics to community social workers, to look at the housing problem from multiple perspectives and provide solutions that will improve living conditions.

Early signs suggest the Healthy Homes Initiative and Warmer Kiwi Homes are performing as planned to improve living conditions in New Zealand homes. An assessment of 250,000 households that received insulation subsidies between 2009 and 2014 as part of Warmer Kiwi Homes found a significant drop in hospital admissions as a result of the intervention, particularly for respiratory conditions.[15] A 2018 evaluation of the Healthy Homes Initiative found that families who received support through the programme felt they were living in warmer, drier and less crowded homes.[16]

Another report in 2019 looked at 1600 households that received support through the initiative and found that there were 160 fewer hospitalisations, 990 fewer GP visits and 920 fewer medicine dispensations from the chemist among this group than would have been the case without the initiative.[17] The Healthy Homes Initiative is estimated to have saved the New Zealand taxpayer around $10 million per year in preventable health care costs, which is about twice the annual cost of the initiative.

The medical and financial benefits of these programmes are undeniable. Less measurable but equally important are the benefits to society that come with moving families from cold and damp housing to warm and dry comfort. Children can do their homework in warm bedrooms instead of near the only heater in a noisy communal space. A mother trying to find a new job can set up an interview because her children are healthy and back at school.

It is too early to tell quantitatively whether programmes such as the Healthy Homes Initiative or Warmer Kiwi Homes have substantially reduced rates of rheumatic fever. However, given the early signs suggesting that hospitalisations and GP visits go down if living conditions are improved, programmes like these may be our best hope of reducing the burden of rheumatic fever over the long term.

∞

New laws set by the New Zealand parliament will intensify building in urban areas.[18] This means the land on which a dwelling sits will shrink. Larger sections within driving distance of the city centre are on the way out, to be replaced by multiple dwellings of the same size on the same inner city site, close to doctors and clinics. On the one hand, you might argue this trend is tearing the fabric of traditional Kiwi life, making the 'half-gallon quarter-acre pavlova paradise' a thing of the past. On the other hand, New Zealand is inexorably transitioning from extensive to intensive land use, which is far better for the environment. Also, good urban design creates public green spaces that serve as our collective backyards. This can be seen in large developments such as Flat Bush in East Auckland, where new high-density housing is built around large public green spaces, with plenty of room for children and adults to exercise and have fun.

The intensification of urban land use is important for combating rheumatic fever. As more housing becomes available, there is a potential for increased affordability, allowing more people to access high-quality, warm, dry homes. This is crucial for Māori and Pacific peoples, the majority of whom live in urban areas[19] but are boxed out of home ownership because of soaring home prices. The Kiwi love affair with the quarter-acre section should be seen as a relic of a bygone era that contributed to the poor quality of urban housing and the severe shortage of affordable dwellings. From this perspective, low-density housing could be perceived as a public health concern that the new regulations will ameliorate.

The government also recently introduced the Public Housing Plan, which aims to deliver 2000 transitional and 6000 public houses, adding nearly 10 percent to the current total number of such dwellings over the coming years.[20] Whether this target will be achieved remains to be seen, but if it is it would represent a substantial investment in safe, warm housing for our most vulnerable children.

In recent years, the government has also shown a willingness to address homelessness. The Housing First initiative, for example, removes barriers to housing support for those with addiction or mental illness.[21] This scheme recognises that when people have a stable, healthy place to live, their addiction and mental health care can be provided more effectively. Creating Positive Pathways is another initiative that provides stable housing, in this case for people leaving prison. It aims to reduce recidivism and homelessness through housing. These interventions also show a commitment to pursuing a kaupapa Māori approach: by Māori, for Māori, with Māori. This makes it more likely that these initiatives will benefit the people who need them most. These efforts on the part of central and local governments are encouraging, acknowledging that housing in New Zealand is unfair and unhealthy, and must change.

These housing interventions funded in New Zealand over the previous decade demonstrate two things. First, it is possible for the government to prioritise investing in improving our housing stock. Second, these investments lead to significant health gains, particularly for children. But each new government has fresh priorities and different constituents to satisfy. Pledging to improve the lot of the most underprivileged people in our population is not necessarily a vote-winning strategy. Yet it is beyond question that better quality housing leads to better health outcomes. Given this relationship, a failure to deliver warm, dry housing to those who need it the most reflects poorly on our values as a society. By extension, I suggest that the reluctance of government to get involved in the housing market perpetuates a crisis in the supply of healthy homes for New Zealand's most vulnerable families.

The undeniable existence of an essential relationship between housing and health should underpin all public debate about this issue and prevent such debate from defaulting to partisan lines. Among the topics that need to be discussed is what to do with the existing, unhealthy properties in the private rental market. Are new regulations required to govern the quality of these properties? If so, what should these regulations be? Should they be a voluntary code, or compulsory? In 2017, the Housing and Health research team at the University of Otago created an example of a rental 'warrant of fitness', which was developed and tested in five regions across New Zealand. It includes a checklist of 29 items that are assessed within a home, granting a 'fail' or 'pass' to each item.[22] The 'warrant' checks, among other things, whether surfaces are free of mould, whether insulation is up to code, whether there are holes in the roof and whether there is effective ventilation. Accredited, independent testers assess a landlord's property and re-assess every three to five years. How effective this programme has been, both in terms of uptake and impact, is overdue for its own assessment. But what if we made this currently voluntary certificate a mandatory part of tenancy agreements?[23] If any items fell below standards, landlords would need to fix them before a follow-up inspection or be in breach of the tenancy agreement.

Another question worth debating is how to get people out of rental accommodation and into their own properties. We could put measures in place to make housing more affordable. For example, we might consider government-guaranteed loans (like the government's current five percent deposit First Home Loan for those with low incomes), which could be expanded so families living in poverty do not have to pay a deposit.[24] And, at the risk of polarising the public quicker than the time it takes to whisper 'capital gains tax', perhaps it is time to revisit how we reduce incentives for property speculation. When housing is in short supply, property speculation as a means of investment increases house prices, creating a feedback loop that places first-home affordability at the mercy of investors.[25] The median house price across New Zealand rose 53% in the 18 months from June 2019 to January 2021, and then dropped again by 20% in the six months to June 2023.[26] If homeownership helps protect against rheumatic fever, and affordable homes can determine people's health, then such rapid fluctuations represent far too much uncertainty.

Given the reality that many low-income families may still be unable to purchase a house, increasing the amount of public rental housing available is also worth investigating. Investment in this type of housing has dropped over the last decade, with the number of state houses (as they are called) owned or managed by the New Zealand government falling from around 70,000 in the early 2010s to around 62,000 by 2020.[27] As the demand for more affordable rental properties has gone up, the supply of state housing has gone down, exacerbating the housing crisis for low-income New Zealanders. Government investment in state housing can be politically polarising, viewed by some as 'nanny-state' meddling. But the other side of the argument is that affordable, high-quality rental accommodation – which state housing should ideally be – supports vulnerable families towards better health and a more productive life. Healthy housing for all should be a right, not a privilege.

One way of avoiding political polarisation around state housing is the recent push toward a public-private model of provision. On the positive side, this approach should reduce the cost burden of state housing for government, and also incentivise the private housing market to produce the kinds of affordable housing that low-income families need. On the negative side, involving private interests in social housing could raise the question of who the house is being built for – the low-income tenant or the high-income landlord. To realise the potential of this model, each public-private partnership must make it clear that low-income families are the true clients of social housing well before ground is broken.

We could also expand the eligibility criteria for community-based programmes like the Healthy Homes Initiative. Evidence on the link between poor housing and the risk of rheumatic fever from the RF RISK study strongly suggests that this would result in fewer cases of rheumatic fever in New Zealand. Currently, budgetary constraints on the programme mean that only those who are suffering severe hardship are eligible to receive support. Half a billion dollars had been spent by 2017 on subsidies to private landlords and owner-occupiers to insulate and heat their homes through the Warmer Kiwi Homes programme.[28] This represents a level of investment far above that granted for the Healthy Homes Initiative and its regional programmes such as AWHI in Auckland and Well Homes in Wellington. More coordination between all the existing housing support programmes, in the spirit of learning from one another's successes and failures, would ensure continuous improvements in the effectiveness and efficiency of help for all vulnerable groups throughout the country.

According to a 2023 Statistics New Zealand report, around 150,000 children – approximately 13 percent of all children – live in severe income poverty in New Zealand.[29] It may seem unrealistic at first, but it should be possible for a well-resourced Healthy Homes Initiative to assess the living conditions of every single one of these children, identify housing problems and then provide the support needed to improve their standard of living. Helping our children thrive should be politically neutral. Any initiative that elevates children's living conditions also elevates the families or caregivers who share their homes. In this scenario, everyone wins.

Chapter Eight
The causes of the causes II: Poverty and power

WHEN I WAS A TEENAGER, close family friends travelled to a developing country. When they came back, my parents invited them for dinner so that we could hear about their adventures. They captivated us with tales of street markets and kind locals – and overwhelming destitution. They described people living in shanties with an almost complete lack of basic infrastructure, without clean drinking water, functioning sewage systems or power. Our friends told us that despite these challenges, the locals seemed a joyful bunch, cheerily content with their lot. The discussion shifted to the differences between the developing world and New Zealand. One of our friends remarked bluntly, 'There's no poverty in New Zealand.' To his mind, the very idea that poverty existed in New Zealand was nonsense.

If I were at that dinner table now, I might ask him a few questions about what he meant. Did the local people our friend met seem kind and happy because in their culture it would have been considered rude to be otherwise in the presence of a visitor? Had he spent much time with people in those shantytowns, or had he mostly spoken with the residents of better-resourced neighbourhoods? At the time, I didn't think to question our guest's claim that New Zealand had no poverty. Still, his remark left a lasting impression. His claim became my truth for the next decade.

Throughout my teens and early twenties, I believed hard work was all that was required to achieve success and that poverty was an avoidable outcome in life. I grew up in a very supportive household, where the prevailing belief was that anyone from anywhere could do anything. This belief sustained me through university and into a career I love. I would learn much later, however, that this belief in self-reliance ignores the fact that success is much easier to achieve if you come from a stable, affluent environment. You cannot pull yourself up by the bootstraps if you have no boots. The truth is that poverty may be absolute, with people battling to survive, as well as relative, with some people within a single country having significantly fewer resources than their more affluent fellow citizens.

Eventually, I came to clearly see the links between poverty and ethnicity in New Zealand, and started to do some thinking of my own. During my postgraduate studies at the University of Auckland, my research focused on diabetes. I reviewed dozens of research articles on the relationship between socioeconomic deprivation and the risk of developing diabetes. I saw that the prominent risk factors for leg amputation among those with diabetes in New Zealand were poverty (both absolute and relative) and having Māori or Pacific Island ethnicity.

One specific episode of fieldwork washed away my assumptions about New Zealand's poverty and its causes. A frequent complication of chronic diabetes is diabetic peripheral neuropathy, or damage to the sensory nerves of (usually) the feet and legs. The hallmarks of peripheral neuropathy are changes in lower-limb sensation and, consequently, balance problems. My doctoral thesis involved testing whether people with this condition would benefit from certain low-impact physical exercises. To draw people into the study, I travelled around South Auckland to patients' homes, explaining what the study involved and asking if they would participate. Nearly all the men and women I visited happily signed up on the spot.

One day, I drove from our laboratory at the university to the home of a potential participant in Ōtara in South Auckland. Ōtara is one of the more deprived urban areas of New Zealand, one I visited frequently when recruiting participants for the project. I had met some wonderful families throughout this suburb and was already working with two Ōtara patients on their twice-weekly, at-home exercises. I knew my way around the area fairly well, but this person's address wasn't familiar to me at all. After pulling over to look at my map, I realised the cul-de-sac I wanted was in the middle of Ōtara, closed in on all sides by housing, and only connected to the rest of the suburb by a labyrinth of smaller streets.

As I took side street after side street towards the heart of the suburb, the age and condition of the housing – which was bad to begin with – visibly deteriorated. On the cul-de-sac where my prospective patient lived, the houses were wooden structures barely recognisable as dwellings. What appeared to be state housing from the 1960s was in abject disrepair. Graffitied plywood covered some holes in the sides of buildings, while others remained gaping.

I drove to the end of the cul-de-sac, followed it around and drove away. Once I had turned onto the next street, I pulled over and called the woman I was meant to meet on my cell phone. I lied and told her I needed to postpone our meeting. I imagined her standing in the front room of her home, looking through a gap in the plywood and wondering if I had been the one driving that silver Honda.

Later that day, I called her and lied again, telling her I had reviewed her file and discovered she did not fit the eligibility criteria for the study. She was disappointed and said she really wanted someone to show her how to stimulate feeling in her legs, but she understood. She wished me well and said she hoped we would learn something to help people like her.

All these years later, I am still ashamed of what I did that day. This book marks the first time I have admitted my actions. I never told my supervisors. At the time, I justified what I had done by telling myself the neighbourhood was unsafe and that I did not want to commit to visiting such a street twice a week for 12 weeks, especially if there were appointments after dark. The reason I remain ashamed is because I think I would still struggle with this decision today. I would still be afraid. I know, deep within myself, that fear for my personal safety might outweigh my desire to meet those most in need on their own turf. Feigning concern for the ugly and dangerous reality of lives lived in poverty and then looking away as quickly as we can seems to be a privilege reserved for the educated middle-class. In this respect, I'm no different to anyone else.

Driving down that cul-de-sac, I realised, in a way I did not in my late teens and early twenties, that real poverty exists in New Zealand.

∞

Poverty is bad for your health. Consider the cascade of negative effects it has on a new baby. Poverty means shoddy housing that is neither warm nor dry, raising the risk of its occupants picking up viral or bacterial illnesses. The newborn child's house may be overcrowded. Perhaps large extended families live under one roof to save money; perhaps everyone gathers in one room to stay warm. The baby born into poverty may have hardly any warm clothes to wear. Their parents may not be able to wash and dry what clothes there are. And the parents may not realise the health risks their new baby faces.

For many reasons, including lower levels of educational achievement, families living in poverty often have reduced factual knowledge about health issues. One day, a child may wake up with a severe sore throat. If the parent lacks the understanding to spot the early signs of strep throat, the illness may be allowed to run its course rather than be subdued with antibiotics. The problems compound: poor health literacy is related to poverty, which in turn often means substandard living conditions – increasing the likelihood that the untreated sore throat might be a *Group-A Strep* infection.

Once the child's health has more obviously deteriorated, the parent may take them to a doctor. Here, more obstacles might present themselves. New Zealand has a publicly funded healthcare system, but there are still some individual costs associated with access to care, such as paying to see a nurse or general practitioner, particularly in an after-hours clinic. Even a few dollars can mean making a choice between taking a child to the doctor or buying food for the family. Transport also poses logistical and financial challenges. Those living in poverty may not own a car, so will need to organise a lift or use public transport (and get themselves and their sick child to the bus stop or train station, which may be blocks away). If the family does own a car, they need to consider fuel and parking costs. If they visit Auckland's Starship Children's Hospital, for instance, parking alone costs at least $20 a day.[1] Pondering whether you'll be able to pay for a park as you are driving your acutely ill child to hospital is another terror for those bouncing on the poverty line. If that child is diagnosed with rheumatic fever, similar obstacles must be faced and somehow overcome for years as children attend the essential regular follow-up appointments for cardiac care and monthly penicillin injections.

Poverty cultivates rheumatic fever, first by engineering the conditions within which *Group-A Strep* can thrive and then by reducing the capacity of those caring for the child to notice and fight the illness. The very things that led to a child's illness will conspire to keep them ill, perhaps for the rest of their life.

∽

Let's consider a parallel universe in which poverty, housing and literacy remain unchanged; but the quality and responsiveness of clinical services are vastly different. The child – let's assume they are a young Māori boy just like Keg – wakes with a sore throat. They complain to their mum, who does not have a strong understanding of the potential importance of the sore throat. However, they do know that their local marae has a walk-in clinic and that it has already opened for the day to serve the community. This is important because the mum needs to go to work later that day and doesn't have the luxury of taking time off whenever an appointment is available.

The mum and her son arrive at the marae and are welcomed into the on-site clinic by familiar faces. Some are relatives, most are friends. All are friendly and well-grounded in tikanga (loosely, 'Māori ways of doing things'). The boy takes a seat next to others in the queue. The aunties (not necessarily by relation) pour cups of coffee or tea, and have a biscuit and a giggle with each other while any paperwork is quickly dealt with.

After a brief wait, mum and son are called into the clinic room. Another friendly face – a Māori nurse or doctor who grew up just down the road, with connection to the whenua (land) and local tikanga. More smiles, more giggles between mum and clinician. A swab is produced, and reassurances are given. The clinician gives a straightforward explanation of the likely problem and outlines the next steps in their plan. A script for antibiotics is given, and the mum and son are told to drop by the on-site pharmacy on their way out. Before they leave, they are asked if they understand what has been discussed during the visit. They are told to come back any time if the symptoms get worse or change.

At the pharmacy, they are greeted by more familiar faces – a Māori pharmacist supported by another aunty. The script is handed over, and antibiotics are swiftly produced. The aunty explains what time to take the medicine, reinforces the need to finish the whole course, and makes a plan for someone from the clinic to call Mum in a few days with the swab result and to see how her son is feeling.

Mum and son leave the clinic, waving goodbye to the aunties. A bill was never produced, and money was never requested – other than perhaps a gold coin koha for the biscuit jar.

A few days later, an aunty calls with the news that the swab result was positive for *Group-A Strep*. She asks if the son is feeling better and double-checks that he is still taking his antibiotics. If there are any further issues, the aunty follows up with the same clinician who saw them in the clinic and helps to arrange further escalation of care.

∽

What are the meaningful features of this parallel universe scenario? Firstly, care was available at a time that worked for the mum and son. Knowing that she could take her son to receive the care he needed without having to book or find a suitable appointment time removed a common barrier to care. The clinic's extended hours meant that Mum could take her son outside of school or work times.

Next, the care was located close to home. Her son didn't need an ambulance or an emergency room; he just needed a check-up and a care plan from someone with high health literacy. That sort of care can be provided anywhere with four walls and a roof.

Next, the environment in which the care was provided was familiar to the mum and son. Being at their local marae meant they understood where to park and the layout of the buildings before they arrived because they had been there many times before. The marae was a 'safe space' where they felt relaxed and at home.

Next, the faces that greeted them when they arrived were also familiar – 'aunties' by blood or in the broader sense of the word. That familiarity removed any residual fear about the clinic visit. Laughter, too, is a powerful medicine that cuts through tension, reduces stigma and lifts spirits. As is true for any given gathering of Māori aunties, the clinic room was full of laughter.

Next, kai (food) was at least part of the clinic visit process. To Māori, kai is more than just a biscuit or a cup of instant coffee. It's a process, a way of connecting and breaking down barriers between people. This is not an unusual concept but rather one that is shared by cultures the world over. Māori are particularly good at incorporating it into all parts of life – so why not include it as part of a clinic visit?

Next, the clinician who provided the check-up and care plan was Māori and local. This is important because she had a shorthand when it came to knowing how to give the best care possible to the mum and son. She understood them because she *was* them. She explained her understanding of the problem and gave a clear plan for how they were going to tackle it together. The mum and son trusted her to a far greater extent than they would likely trust someone who was non-Māori and not a local. That trust would invariably lead to improved adherence to treatment and improved likelihood of return care-seeking if the symptoms got worse.

Next, the pharmacy was on-site, so there was no additional travel to get the antibiotics. Using a te ao Māori worldview, where all things are interconnected, the siloing of our pharmacies away from our clinics makes very little sense. Anyone who accesses primary care in New Zealand knows that we often need to travel – sometimes several kilometres – between a clinic where a script was written and the pharmacy where it can be filled. This is like paying for your groceries at one supermarket and then having to pick them up from another.

Finally, at no point was there any discussion about money. By making the clinic visit and the antibiotics completely free, cost was largely removed as a barrier to care. The location of the clinic just down the road and the extended opening hours also reduce costs associated with travel and meant that Mum didn't need to take time off work or miss out on wages. The marae – and, by extension, the health system that funds the clinic – eliminated all costs because they understand the needs of the highly deprived community they serve. They view providing free care not as an expense but as an investment in the health of their community.

∽

This might all seem fanciful, but it isn't fantasy. In fact, there are pockets of excellence already in operation that share many of these best-practice qualities. In 2023, Māori GP Lance O'Sullivan helped launch Te Whare Oranga, an all-Māori, not-for-profit, nurse-led clinic in Kaitaia, where O'Sullivan will serve as a 'virtual GP' when needed.[2] Māori GP Dr Matire Harwood and colleagues run a medical centre out of Papakura Marae in South Auckland, serving the primary healthcare needs of the marae's local community in a culturally safe and responsive space.[3] Other services provided by the marae include Tamariki Ora, a child health service, and other services aimed at connecting their community to the social determinants of good health, like housing.[4]

Among its impressive list of services, Papakura Marae includes the Mana Kidz school-based programme, which aims to prevent the spread of *Group-A Strep* and rheumatic fever in the South Auckland community via school-based intervention. Mana Kidz is run by the National Hauora Coalition, a Māori primary care organisation.[5] The programme targets schools in high-deprivation areas, offering wrap-around care that includes managing sore throats and skin infections, and conducting ear, vision and general wellness checks. Since children spend most of their time at home or school, embedding primary care in communities and educational settings seems highly complementary.

From the moment of *Group-A Strep* transmission, the clock is ticking. Delivering primary care close to where people spend the majority of their time and ensuring that care is delivered by familiar faces in a familiar environment invariably reduces the kinds of barriers to care that matter in the context of rheumatic fever.

∞

It is tempting to view financial success as a result of one's own initiative and ambition, as I once did. From this perspective, poor people just need to roll up their sleeves and get to work. The financial rewards will follow. In New Zealand, this view received publicity when John Key was elected Prime Minister in 2008. Raised by a single mother in a state house in Christchurch, Key's humble beginnings became part of his political brand. In his maiden speech to parliament in 2002, Key leaned into his personal history. 'When I was six,' he related, 'my father died, leaving my mother penniless with three children to raise. From a humble start in a state house, she worked as a cleaner and night porter until she earned the deposit for a modest home. She was living testimony that you get out of life what you put into it. There is no substitute for hard work and determination. These are the attitudes she instilled in me.'[6]

Key's tale is indeed remarkable. He excelled in secondary school and then at the University of Canterbury, where he studied commerce and accounting. Then he entered financial management, first in New Zealand, then in Singapore, Australia and London. By the time he ran for parliament, this son of a porter had amassed a personal fortune. He had started with nothing, worked hard and earned his success.

Believing in the direct link between individual action and financial success, or in the economic meritocracy, is seductive. It is easy to frame our financial circumstances as being within our control and thus intrinsically modifiable. A better future awaits us, but only if we want it enough and are prepared to work for it. Key's narrative won him praise on talk radio, votes on the hustings and victory on election day.

However, personal ambition and action do not necessarily lead directly to financial reward. Those born into poor households face many more barriers to financial success than those in the middle and upper classes. In New Zealand, the likelihood of starting with nothing is strongly determined by ethnicity: 25 percent of Māori and 35 percent of Pacific New Zealanders live in the most deprived neighbourhoods in New Zealand, compared to less than five percent of New Zealand Europeans.[7]

Key may have clawed his way out of poverty, but as humble as his beginnings were, he also grew up a male European in Anglocentric Christchurch. These were significant advantages in 1970s New Zealand. For a meritocracy to work, everyone needs the same opportunities to succeed. In New Zealand, as in other countries struggling with deep inequalities in health and wealth, equal opportunity does not exist. Rather, financial success is at best predicated on and at worst dictated by the circumstances into which we are born.

Key's narrative about his path to success is dangerous because it brushes away social inequality by suggesting we are all masters of our circumstances. It directs attention away from inherently asymmetrical power structures towards individual responsibility. In reality, both are intertwined. Key's message was popular with voters who were already financially successful. It offered them absolution and the assurance that their success was of their own making. For these voters, policies such as low corporate and capital gains taxes are critical to sustaining a meritocracy. Investment in social housing and welfare programmes is worthy of suspicion. Why help the disadvantaged when all they have to do is try harder?

The power of the meritocracy narrative is important to understanding the social determinants of rheumatic fever. Key's government implemented the Rheumatic Fever Prevention Programme (RFPP) in 2011, but the bulk of the funding was directed at goals to be achieved within only one or two election cycles. Abolishing generations of obstacles to good health is only possible if we take the long view. Executing a long-term strategic plan to address the social determinants of rheumatic fever and other poverty-related diseases means looking carefully at our social paradigms and then slowly undoing certain foundational assumptions, including our seductive belief that a fortune awaits all who work hard.

∽

Bringing about meaningful change to the systems underpinning a society is challenging. In New Zealand, political power to effect change comes down to winning enough votes in a general election, ideally enough to form a majority government. Rheumatic fever, however, is a minority disease. Convincing the 68 percent of New Zealanders who are of European descent that we need to address the system-level factors causing a disease that almost exclusively affects Māori (18 percent of New Zealanders) and Pacific peoples (nine percent) is difficult.[8] Promoting policies to eliminate the social determinants of rheumatic fever probably will not win an election; placing such policies at the core of a party manifesto could lose one.

In New Zealand, those who do not hold power are disproportionately affected by the social determinants of health. The sheer number of European votes ensures that Māori and Pacific needs are likely to be the last to be considered. Issues important to these groups are typically addressed as part of broader policy packages or, in the case of the Māori Party and the Rheumatic Fever Prevention Programme (RFPP), used as negotiation chips in coalition bargaining. When in

2008 the Māori Party agreed to create a coalition government with the National Party, it did so on the condition that rates of rheumatic fever would be substantially cut through central and regional action.[9] As a result, steps toward the RFPP were set in motion, and a sector of the government's Ministry of Health was designated to advance the programme.

In March 2018, I attended a national workshop hosted by New Zealand's Ministry of Health on the prevention of rheumatic fever. The venue was the Holiday Inn near Auckland's international airport. The hotel rises from a concrete industrial park at a busy intersection, its tropical flair incongruous with its drab setting. The main foyer is like that of any waterfront hotel in Waikiki, but this is the heart of South Auckland, one of the poorest areas in the city. The place feels more like a denial of reality than a whimsical oasis.

The primary goal of the workshop was to bring everyone working in rheumatic fever prevention and care to one place, and to do some knowledge-sharing. The RFPP team had flown in from Wellington to share their key findings from the programme, and our RF RISK team, led by Professor Michael Baker, was there in force. Among the audience were nurses, doctors, academics and community social workers – all working tirelessly on their own piece of New Zealand's rheumatic fever puzzle.

The workshop began with an overview of the RFPP. There was considerable interest in the initiative's throat swabbing programme, which, as noted earlier, had absorbed much of the RFPP's time and funding between 2011 and 2017. The big question was whether these clinics, dedicated to identifying and treating *Group-A Strep* throat infections, had resulted in a measurable difference to rheumatic fever rates. The answer, according to the Ministry of Health team presenting the data, was that although there had been a short-lived decline in cases, the throat swabbing programme's overall success was debatable. This result chimed with the results from our RF RISK study, which Professor Baker revealed for the first time at the next session. Our study had shown that belonging to a school in which the throat swabbing programme had been in operation did *not* reduce the risk of rheumatic fever.

Then came the awkward observation that the decline in rates of rheumatic fever had occurred not only in children of primary and intermediate school age, but also in older children who weren't in the programme. If school-based swabbing had made the difference, then why would rates decline in those who had not participated in the programme? Was it because fewer *Group-A Strep* bacteria had circulated in the community? And if this was so, was it because *Group-A Strep* had increasingly been treated with antibiotics among high-risk communities?

Or was it just coincidence?

Advocates advocated; academics argued.

But at any rate, by the time of the 2018 Holiday Inn workshop, the RFPP, including its throat swabbing programme, had already been wound down. The intervention had shown some positive results: rates of rheumatic fever in regions with the RFPP had dropped by 23 percent. This was well short of the 66 percent promised, but a reduction nonetheless.[10] In the Counties-Manukau region, a flashpoint for the disease, rheumatic fever rates had dropped by more than 30 percent, although they appear to have bounced back since. Driven by local leadership, the RFPP programme continued to operate in nearly 90 schools around Counties Manukau and is still going strong in the region at the time of writing in 2024.

Successive workshop sessions at the Holiday Inn that day made some things very clear. An important lesson from the RFPP is that trying to prevent rheumatic fever by early detection of *Group-A Strep* infections is a tactically complex project. It may never be practical to roll out a homogenous throat-swabbing programme capable of capturing every New Zealand case of *Group-A Strep* occurring among school-aged children. Even at the height of the RFPP, only around half of all children in poorer neighbourhoods attended a school with a throat swabbing programme. It was left to the district health boards involved in the RFPP to decide which schools within their district would run the programme, with some selected based on the rate of rheumatic fever in their area, and others based on the deprivation decile of the school. Counties Manukau District Health Board, for example, used a scoring system based on the rheumatic fever rate of the area surrounding the school, the number of rheumatic fever cases within a school, the decile of the school and the proportion of the school roll that was made up of Māori or Pacific students.[11] On top of this variable school selection system, the ideal of national homogeneity often clashed with the need for local pragmatism. Some schools ran swabbing clinics every school day, some did not. Some swabbed for skin infections as well as throat infections, some did not.

The story of the RFPP showed something else, too: the profound sense of unity and purpose shared by community health workers when striving towards a common goal on the frontline of a public health crisis. Passion for the fight against rheumatic fever was palpable in every conversation I had, from nurses taking throat swabs to project managers of health service providers to paediatricians leading the clinical charge. The RFPP taught us that if you set clear goals and secure resources to achieve them, capable people join the fight.

Yet, leaving the dreary conference room for the palm-lined car park, I was confused. I had just attended an all-day workshop with the brightest and most passionate minds in rheumatic fever prevention in New Zealand, whose goal was to settle on a plan to eliminate this disease. But underpinning every session was the knowledge that the RFPP had recently been almost completely defunded. This Holiday Inn workshop had really been to sum up a now-extinct programme – a frustratingly inconclusive summary. Most workshop participants – myself included – were left with many questions. Rates of rheumatic fever had dipped during the RFPP, but we did not know why. Rates were climbing again, including in districts that had school-based throat clinics, and again we did not know why. The findings of our RF RISK study would soon be public, providing evidence-based reasons for the government to invest in raising housing standards and reducing poverty. But with the RFPP no longer operating in nearly all districts, most of the experienced people in the Ministry of Health's rheumatic fever task force would be redeployed to other projects. How would further positive change now happen?

Two years after that Holiday Inn workshop, as the first cases of COVID-19 arrived in New Zealand in 2020, rates of rheumatic fever had largely returned to pre-RFPP levels. The original goal of the RFPP had been to reduce rates to 1.4 per 100,000 New Zealanders by 2017. But by 2020, the rate remained relatively steady at around three per 100,000.[12] In 2023, rates among Māori and Pacific peoples appeared to have reduced over time from pre-RFPP levels, and to still be falling slowly. But because of the relatively rare nature of the disease overall, an additional 10 to 20 Māori or Pacific cases in any given year could completely change our interpretation of this trend. For example, the rate of rheumatic fever among Pacific peoples in 2020 was 19 per 100,000; in 2021 it dropped to eight per 100,000; and by 2022 it was back up to 19 per 100,000. Even if there are signals that rheumatic fever rates might be slowly reducing, they remain well shy of the original RFPP goal in 2011 of reducing the incidence of rheumatic fever by two thirds within five years. We are even further away from eliminating rheumatic fever altogether.

Without funding, much of the national momentum gained around the primary prevention of rheumatic fever was lost. It was left to those same clinicians, academics, community workers and stakeholders who had been roused to action by the RFPP to create a Māori- and Pacific-led advocacy group – Pū Manawa – to continue the fight for a more coordinated and better-resourced response to rheumatic fever.[13] Pū Manawa work with the government to plan future activities around rheumatic fever and rheumatic heart disease prevention and treatment. Pū Manawa's vision is a rheumatic fever- and rheumatic heart disease-free New Zealand. In 2023, the government published a rheumatic fever 'roadmap', which includes strong support for action around the social determinants of rheumatic fever, including housing.[14] Whether the government uses the roadmap to drive policy and resource allocation remains to be seen.

When the RFPP was set up in 2011, the government created a pitfall for itself – not by saying it would cut rates of rheumatic fever, but by claiming it would cut them by two thirds in *five* years. This hefty promise needed a quick and well-organised mobilisation of forces and funds. However, rheumatic fever is a persistent problem that requires ongoing attention and money. The knowledge gleaned from our RF RISK study, unavailable when the RFPP was launched, suggests that instead of investing $65 million to treat our way out of rheumatic fever by eliminating *Group-A Strep* when it was already in the throats and on the skin of our children, it would be more fruitful to go after the causes of the cause – that is, the environmental factors that allow *Group-A Strep* to thrive: poverty and poor-quality housing.

∞

The Child Poverty Reduction Act became law in 2018. It is perhaps the most important law ever passed to address children's health in New Zealand.[15] In some ways, this legislation is at the heart of the rheumatic fever story. It recognises that New Zealand has significant poverty that ruins the lives of children and that we must end it.

As the bill passed through various readings before becoming an Act of Parliament, data regarding child poverty surfaced. A University of Otago report found that 15 percent of New Zealand children (some 150,000) were living in material hardship with restricted access to such necessities as shoes, water and electricity.[16] That 15 percent of Kiwi children were living in deprivation was apparently difficult to vote against. This may explain why the bill enjoyed almost unanimous support in a diverse parliament, passing 119 votes to one.

The Act requires that a sitting government must strive to halve child poverty within 10 years of signing. Whatever party leads the government, it needs to set three- and 10-year targets to reduce child poverty so that, whether or not this issue is a priority, the sitting government must act. The goal is to reduce the percentage of children living in material hardship from 15 to seven percent and the proportion of children living in low-income households from 20 to 10 percent by 2028. Since Māori and Pacific children make up a disproportionate number of those living in poverty, these groups stand to benefit.

In truth, the Child Poverty Reduction Act was a piece of legislative subterfuge. Reducing material hardship for children improves adults' lives, too. The minority-led government at the time focused on children to rally those who would typically oppose government action against poverty. By fashioning a bill that would force current and future governments to monitor and act on childhood poverty, the government mustered support for a law that, in effect, would tackle poverty overall.

Since the Act was passed, child poverty has declined. Progress has been slow but solving an issue as complex as poverty will take time. Benefits emerging from the Act, such as funding boosts for families with low incomes, providing school lunches in poor neighbourhoods and waiving medical fees for children under 14, make a meaningful difference. Such benefits need to be a permanent part of the fight against poverty.

The Child Poverty Reduction Act is a decisive victory in the fight against rheumatic fever. Even better, this law will probably be impervious to political change. The overwhelming support it received in parliament is the strongest illustration of humane decision-making we have seen in generations. We have reason to be hopeful.

Alongside the child poverty legislation, 2018 also saw the beginnings of significant changes to the landscape of New Zealand healthcare. In May, the New Zealand government announced a review of New Zealand's health and disability services. After a long and winding review process, and backed by new 'health in all policies' legislation (known as the Pae Ora Act), sweeping reforms to New Zealand's health and disability service delivery were rolled out across 2022. A year later, three new government agencies – the Māori Health Authority, Health NZ and the Public Health Agency – were up and running. The Māori Health Authority – Te Aka Whai Ora – was disbanded by the incoming government after less than two years of operation in early 2024.

What might these health reforms mean for rheumatic fever?

Firstly, Health NZ was created to replace the district health board model, where 20 boards around the country were funding and delivering care in a largely devolved way. Housing support, sore throat clinics and services that deliver antibiotics to rheumatic fever sufferers had all been funded through the local district health board and other stakeholders. This funding was precariously dependent on how highly a given board or stakeholder group valued the work. Theoretically, as opposed to introducing such interventions piecemeal, Health NZ would lead to more centralised health planning and delivery. This could allow us to take lessons from local successes, reproduce them to scale and then roll them out to the whole country. The remnants of the RFPP still operating in South Auckland are an example of such a programme. What is happening in South Auckland could be reproduced in other regions where rheumatic fever is common. Centralisation of care could help to share and spread good ideas. But centralisation could also put such programmes at risk if they were not seen as valuable or scalable, since the natural enemy of centralisation is regional variation.

Secondly, the creation of a dedicated Public Health Agency means that, in theory, we can use public health data to help us nationally monitor and fight rheumatic fever. This data has been missing from treatment plans, while researchers outside of government have provided much of the information on the disease. Studies like RF RISK should not be dependent on a few researchers and clinicians championing the cause and securing research funding. The Public Health Agency is well suited to monitor how common rheumatic fever is and how rates are distributed by ethnicity and other demographic and geographic factors.

The closure of the Māori Health Authority is a blow to interventions that directly help Māori. By extension, this closure also affects Pacific peoples, since they often share the environments that drive high rates of rheumatic fever among Māori. Initiatives such as marae- or church-based programmes to treat skin infections in young children,[17] or a Māori- and Pacific-focused antibiotic prophylaxis service more appealing than the current model,[18] will need to be developed by one or more other agencies within our health system.

Health system reforms cause substantial upheaval, and those living through them cannot see their full downstream impact. As with all interventions that may directly or indirectly affect rheumatic fever, whether the current upheaval will improve the prevention and care of this disease will only become clear with time.

Chapter Nine
The path forward

THE PREVIOUS CHAPTERS have discussed the causes of rheumatic fever, from biology to social determinants and everything in between. We know that the conditions that give rise to the proliferation and spread of *Group-A Strep* also give rise to rheumatic fever. We know that a household with poor health literacy is less likely to seek treatment for a *Group-A Strep* infection, meaning that health education (and education in general) plays a role in rheumatic fever development. We know that even after taking account of differences in health literacy, children who go on to develop rheumatic fever are more likely to have faced barriers in getting into primary care than those who don't. This means that we also have work to do to improve timely primary care access for those at risk of rheumatic fever.

We know that the best way to reduce barriers to healthcare is to bring that care to the people who need it. We already have excellent examples of this in action, such as the medical centre run out of Papakura Marae and the nurse-led centre running in Kaitaia.[1] De-siloing care wherever possible and delivering it close to where people live, in a familiar environment – whether that be a marae, church or community centre – will reduce barriers to the delivery of care.

While most cases of rheumatic fever will occur following a throat infection, we now know that skin infection is another vector: for children at high risk of rheumatic fever, early treatment and elimination of *Group-A Strep* from skin sores should theoretically be as routine as treating a throat infection.

We know that household crowding, whether around heating sources or through child bed-sharing, drives *Group-A Strep* spread within families as well as rheumatic fever development. This has broader ramifications in terms of the need to reduce child poverty and more specific ramifications around housing insulation, heating and hot water access. We know that poor-quality housing leads to rheumatic fever development and, conversely, that access to high-quality housing is protective. There are programmes that are addressing much of these housing-related issues, and these programmes are scalable. We could expand the Healthy Homes Initiative in New Zealand to target all families living in poverty. This initiative has already improved health outcomes and is cost-effective. It just needs funding commensurate with its task.

We know that it matters whether you own or rent your house, and if you rent your house, it matters who you rent it from. Making home ownership more affordable for the underprivileged could be transformative for reducing rheumatic fever. As of 2024, even a below-average first home in South Auckland costs at least $800,000, meaning $40,000, if the buyer qualified, is the best deposit rate that these buyers can hope for. I'm certain the Ōtara client I shamefully neglected during my PhD study would need a lifetime to save that much money. We have the power to give her and her children the option of living in their own home without requiring a deposit, and with a manageable interest rate to service. Why not use it?

∽

The interventions summarised above would go some way toward eliminating rheumatic fever. These changes would require a significant allocation of resources, making them easy to talk about but difficult to implement. Enacting social change is hard: gathering support for that change is harder, particularly given who the change is for.

Consider the following thought experiment. Say I discover a childhood ailment called 'Gurney's Disease' that is caused by prolonged exposure to hot and dry conditions. Let's say the disease is characterised by severe swelling of children's hearts and possible permanent damage to their fragile cardiac valves. Adults die as a result of their childhood encounters with Gurney's Disease. The disease almost exclusively impacts New Zealand's European population, with rates 20 times higher than in the Māori population and around 50 times higher than in the Pacific population. We know that by creating more shaded spaces and interiors with air conditioning we would dramatically reduce the rate of the disease.

If Gurney's Disease were real and affected European children more than Māori or Pacific peoples (setting aside economic disparities), I have little doubt that it would be a core election issue. The party with the most convincing plan for its elimination would win. If this scenario seems far-fetched, consider Labour's landslide victory in the 2020 general election as it led the response to the COVID-19 pandemic, which threatened to kill New Zealanders of all ethnicities.

In New Zealand, more than two thirds of the population is of European descent. The recent Health and Disability System Review identified that a system like ours, intended to work for the greatest number of people, seems to be either passively or actively designed primarily for our European population.[2] Having this model means that our system does not respond well to the health needs of the minority populations it is supposed to serve, which is particularly problematic when our citizens with the biggest health problems are

Māori and Pacific peoples. For example, despite Māori comprising 18 percent of the population, Māori make up only four percent of general practitioners (GPs).[3] Pacific peoples represent nine percent of the population but only three percent of GPs. The same shortage is seen in the proportion of paediatricians, the main doctors who will treat children diagnosed with rheumatic fever (four percent Māori, three percent Pacific).

As noted earlier, a European living in New Zealand with rheumatic heart disease will live, on average, more than 20 years longer than a Māori or Pacific person with the same disease.[4] Māori with rheumatic heart disease die around 15 years earlier than Māori in the general population (around 60 years compared to around 75). In comparison, Europeans with rheumatic heart disease die only three years earlier than Europeans in the general population (around 80 years compared to around 83).[5] This disproportionate life expectancy between peoples with the same disease strongly suggests that our system is underperforming for Māori (and Pacific) peoples.

The fact that rheumatic fever and its causes have not had a strong presence in our political conversations since the end of the RFPP is almost certainly because of ethnicity. The closure of the Māori Heath Authority before it had a chance to flourish signals that attempts to address Māori health issues through government-backed, Māori-led action remain divisive in New Zealand. We find it difficult to collectively agree that ethnicity might be both a direct and indirect cause of poor health outcomes, unless that cause is genetic. Just as there are patterns of genetic diseases within ethnic groups that have shared ancestry, social diseases like rheumatic fever also show patterns within ethnic groups that have a shared social history. Why do we intuitively grasp the former but collectively struggle with the latter?

While Gurney's Disease is an invention, there is a real-world example of a condition that affects significantly more Europeans than Māori or Pacific peoples: skin cancer. The rate of melanoma is around 50 times higher among Europeans than it is among Māori and around 300 times higher than in Pacific peoples.[6] More than 300 Europeans die per year in New Zealand from melanoma, compared to less than 10 Māori and Pacific peoples combined. To prevent skin cancer, we (wisely) invest strongly in things like sunscreen and Sun Smart programmes. When someone is diagnosed with skin cancer, we treat them: in 2021 alone, we spent around $180 million on such treatments.[7] These prevention programmes and treatments will almost exclusively benefit Europeans, but when advocate groups call for further funding of an expensive melanoma medicine, no one calls them racist. When a political leader on the hustings promises that their party will fund the new melanoma medicine, no one calls it a race-based policy. And yet it is, in all but name. The advocate and the politician can avoid basing their argument around ethnic disparities because the issue they are talking about impacts the 68 percent of New Zealanders who are European – the majority. Assuming their case is well-made, both the advocate and the politician will win by sheer weight of support, never having to utter the words 'European' or 'ethnicity'.

In his 2006 book *The Audacity of Hope*, American President Barack Obama observed that to garner majority support for legislation that might only improve the lot of the minority, that legislation must represent the desires and longings of all people.[8] The context of his comment was a nation built on slavery, with an ensuing strong and public history of overt (and often violent) racism. Applying Obama's logic to New Zealand would involve framing the fight against rheumatic fever as defending *all* children's wellbeing, not just *Māori and Pacific* children's wellbeing. Maybe this would work; the melanoma example suggests that it might. But there is a deeper question that we may need to answer before we can make true progress toward eliminating rheumatic fever: why do we need to reframe an issue in order to justify action just because it only impacts Māori and Pacific peoples? What does that say about us?

∞

So, while we already have clear evidence to back the kind of social change needed to eliminate rheumatic fever, there is a lack of widespread support for this change. However, there are plenty of unanswered questions that require our attention while we wait for the will for change to grow.

Firstly, there is a need to firmly establish the skin infection–rheumatic fever pathway in the minds of policy-makers, clinicians and the public. Making sure policy-makers are aware of this link has ramifications for how we organise our system to deal with skin infections, spanning everything from clinical guidelines to the level of public funding of swabbing and treatment. Making sure clinicians, particularly primary care clinicians, understand this link has ramifications in delivering that care. And making sure the public understands this link has ramifications in terms of care-seeking: where once a skin infection might be ignored, linking that infection to more serious outcomes could improve timely access to care. This will need to be balanced against potentially driving public panic over every cut and scrape. Therefore, understanding the best approach to public education of this pathway is an important area of research.

Growing fears of antibiotic resistance are heightening the focus on their appropriate use, a movement known as antibiotic stewardship. This means that it isn't always straightforward to prescribe antibiotics without a positive swab (throat or skin), which has ramifications in terms of the timely eradication of *Group-A Strep*. The current Heart Foundation guidelines suggest that antibiotics should be given in primary care without waiting for evidence of a positive swab if the patient is at high risk of rheumatic fever (for example, Māori or Pacific peoples with a family history of rheumatic fever).[9] In my experience as the Māori son of a Māori father with rheumatic heart disease, these guidelines are variably enforced. I remember my mum having to stand her ground and more-or-less demand penicillin from a doctor when I presented with a broken-glass sore throat because she knew the guidelines better than the doctor did. My wife Sarah and I had to do the same with our children. Understanding whether we are under-, over- or appropriately treating suspected *Group-A Strep* infections would tell us how we are tracking and show us where we can do better.

For those children where we cannot prevent rheumatic fever, we can at least try our best to stop them from getting the disease again. Stopping rheumatic fever recurrence reduces the chance of a child having significant rheumatic heart disease in later life. As noted earlier, the way that we currently do this is through painful intramuscular injections of penicillin (usually in the buttock), once every month until the child with rheumatic fever has grown into an adult. It is easy to see why accessing this type of prophylactic treatment is not high on the list of priorities for a child or young adult, and why adherence to this demanding regime can be variable. Variable prophylaxis translates to variable protection against rheumatic fever recurrence.

A recent University of Otago study successfully trialled a new way of delivering prophylactic penicillin to at-risk children: shifting the injection site away from big muscles to fatty tissue just below the skin makes the experience much less painful, and boosting the dose makes it last longer – meaning quarterly instead of monthly injections.[10] Another promising development is implantable antibiotic delivery systems, which eliminate the need for regular injections.[11] These systems are similar to those used by people with Type-1 diabetes to automate their insulin control. Research is crucial to understand the obstacles preventing the widespread adoption of either the new quarterly protocols or the promising implantable technology.

Finally, we must return to the long shadow and the 20-year gap in life expectancy between Māori and Pacific peoples with rheumatic heart disease and their European counterparts. Understanding the drivers of this difference will unlock pathways toward bridging the gap. Are we providing the same level of antibiotic prophylaxis to our Māori and Pacific children following their first bout of rheumatic fever as we are to our European children? Is the life expectancy gap related to the greater comorbidity burden experienced by Māori and Pacific peoples, and if so, how can we optimise comorbidity management among those with rheumatic heart disease to compensate? Are we providing the same heart surveillance and treatment to our Māori and Pacific peoples with rheumatic heart disease as we are to Europeans with the same disease? If not, why not?

In August 2024, Keg turned 69. As a Māori man with rheumatic heart disease, he's beating the odds when it comes to life expectancy. Instrumental in this success has been the ongoing, precise care provided by his cardiologist – the same cardiologist that usually zapped his heart back into rhythm after those flying midnight trips to Middlemore Hospital. For the past 20-plus years, Keg has been paying a considerable sum of money to see that cardiologist in their private practice to avoid waiting lists for check-ups and skip the queues into complex surgery.

Keg's longevity is a success when it comes to the miracles of modern medicine, but a sad indictment on how well our public system works for those with rheumatic heart disease who can't afford private care. Which begs a question that is perhaps the scariest for any country with universal healthcare to answer: to what extent is the 20-year life expectancy gap driven by an unspoken 'class system', where the haves are treated ahead of the have-nots?

Epilogue

IN EARLY 2014 I was on a plane, flying from Auckland to Whangārei with Professor Dinny Lennon. We were on our way to Whangārei Hospital to talk to clinicians about the RF RISK study and, we hoped, gain their support. Professor Lennon and I had taken this trip several times and had come to enjoy each other's company. She knew my father had been in and out of hospital in his fight against rheumatic heart disease. She knew I was on that plane for reasons beyond my professional interest in public health or my personal desire for job security.

After the plane had touched down in Whangārei, it had to wait on the tarmac until permission was given for passengers to disembark. My conversation with Professor Lennon turned to the job at hand. She mentioned how rife rheumatic fever was in Northland at that time. Many children, she said, had been arriving at Whangārei Hospital with serious cardiac symptoms. This is the same hospital Keg had visited for his cardiac scans in 1969 and where I had been born thirteen years later.

Professor Lennon was gazing out the window as she made a chilling observation. 'Those kids,' she said, 'will never make old bones.'

She had made the comment to no one in particular. I knew her words weren't supposed to land so heavily on my chest, but as soon as they were said, my mind sprang straight to my dad and how he might not make old bones.

∽

I have a strong memory of a particular Saturday from my childhood. I was 14 years old, the same age as Keg at the start of his rheumatic fever battle, and proudly following in his footsteps by playing rugby for Hora Hora RFC. That Saturday we were playing the formidable Kauri Coast RFC on their home turf. It was the semi-finals of our local competition, and beating Kauri Coast away from home was all that stood between us and a coveted place in the grand final. We had a talented team, ample spirit and strong leaders. Keg was even the assistant coach, and I can still picture him drilling the backs, teaching them all the tricks and moves he had mastered when he was a young halfback.

Playing Kauri Coast at home had become the stuff of legend. The parochial crowd, the biased refereeing, and the way their players would sharpen their boot sprigs to ensure blood was drawn if you ever found yourself on the wrong side of a ruck. (I still have the lines on my back from that semi-final to this day.) There was no disputing that Kauri Coast were the straight-up thugs of the competition, a reputation they embraced with vigour.

On the long drive from Whangārei out to Kauri Coast, Dad tried to quell my fears with his classic wisdom – reminding me that 'the bigger they are, the harder they fall', and other greatest hits from the Old School Dad album like 'they all poo sitting down'. I never bought the first saying since it was also true that 'the bigger they are, the more it is going to hurt when they smash you'. But I remember that the poo-related one did provide some slight comfort. I told myself that at least when you're getting pummelled by one of the Kauri Coast players, you can always imagine them on the loo with a bad case of diarrhoea.

We finally arrived at Kauri Coast RFC. After the pre-match warm-up and routines, it was game time. Almost immediately, all of the fears that had forced acid water out of my bottom before the match started coming true. And then some.

Not once in the rest of my lacklustre rugby career – which ended with a blown shoulder just a few years later – did I play in a more violent game. We may have only been 14, but I swear that some of these Kauri Coast kids were so big that they had full-grown beards. We had played them before, at our formidable home ground, and won comfortably – but it was like the team we were playing had grown another foot, both up and out. It didn't help that the referee seemed to be playing for them too, or that the linesmen (both Kauri Coast supporters) appeared to be adding 10 metres to each sideline kick from them and subtracting 10 from ours. The boldness of the bias would have been laughable if we hadn't been so determined to grab that spot in the final.

With about 10 minutes to go in the match and with us ahead by a point or so, I was called to the sideline to give one of our reserves some time on the pitch. I was relieved for the break. It had been the most gruelling hour-and-a-bit of footy I'd ever played. Dripping in sweat and with blood seeping through the back of my shirt from the sprig-shivs, I grabbed my bottle of water and took my place on the sideline next to Dad. He told me how proud he was of me, like he always did, then, under his breath, he muttered that he was glad Mum hadn't come to watch today. There was something about seeing her children being beaten to a pulp that Mum didn't seem to appreciate.

With two minutes to play, we were defending a strong attack from Kauri Coast close to our line. All of a sudden, a scuffle broke out amid a ruck that had formed and, by the looks of it, our halfback Harry was in the thick of it. The Kauri Coast boys started pushing him around and, once the pushing started, our boys started pushing back.

Here's the thing about a rugby team, or any competitive sports team for that matter: they might not all get along all the time, but they're essentially large extended families. Weeks of pre-season training, followed by an arduous three-month season of mostly tough games, inevitably breeds a strong sense of unity. My teammate might not always be the kind of person that I would want to spend time with outside of rugby, but once we step on that field together, we're brothers. And if you push my brother, I'm going to push you back.

It doesn't really matter who threw the first punch; it may have been Harry, or it might have been one of the Kauri Coast players. But what does matter is what happened next. Like a flame to tinder, the circle around Harry erupted in flaying arms and fists. He was taking a pummelling, with three or four blue Kauri Coast jerseys whacking away at him. Our boys started punching back, and our captain flew over to the melee from one of the wings. As he ran, he began screaming: 'Ninety-nine!! Ninety-nine!!'

The '99' call is a unique piece of rugby heritage. It started in the 1970s after a particularly brutal British Lion's tour of South Africa, after which it permeated through rugby circles the world over. The original British Lion's call was '999' – an homage to their telephone number for emergency services – but was quickly shortened to '99' when they realised that '999' took too long to say in the heat of battle. Roughly translated, '99' means 'one in, all in' – with the premise being that a referee will find it difficult to send off one particular player for punching if everyone on the team is doing the same thing.

The truth was that I'd never been involved in a 99 before. I'd been in plenty of minor dust-ups and loads of expletive-filled pushing and shoving, but nothing like an all-in brawl. Being so hyped up with the tight game and fearing for my friend, I started to run onto the field as soon I heard the 99 call. In retrospect, I should have left the brawling for those on the pitch. But I was 14 and didn't have any experience or sense. So I ran on.

About 10 metres into my run toward the action, I was sharply grabbed from the side and thrown to the ground.

By the time I had realised what had happened, I was on my back staring up at the largest man I had ever seen. He must have been two metres tall, and he was cussing me out for stepping onto the field. As I tried to get up, he grabbed me by the collar, fiercely twisting my jersey around my neck as he continued to ream me out. I remember feeling intensely frightened, partly because I couldn't breathe properly but mostly because I was worried about what the enormous man was going to do to me next.

And then it happened.

Flying across from the right side of my vision came a blur, a shape moving so fast that I couldn't catch focus. POW! A sudden violent shudder and I fell to the ground again. The enormous man's hand was no longer around the scruff of my neck, and air filled my lungs. Sitting up, I turned to see my dad gripping the collar of the enormous man's shirt.

To appreciate this situation properly, you have to understand a little bit about Keg's physical attributes. He weighs around 85kg and stands at about 1.75m tall (on a good day). The enormous man was an easy 110kg and stood around two metres. It was a welterweight versus heavyweight scenario – David versus Goliath but with no slingshot in sight.

So there's my dad, with his hand stretched skywards around the enormous man's collar. He's walking backwards because the enormous man wasn't about to back down to a David, so he's constantly advancing on him. As he is walked backwards, Dad mutters to the enormous man in a low, menacing tone, saying the same thing over and over: 'Don't you *dare* touch my son. Don't you *dare* touch my son. Don't you *dare* touch my son.'

I don't know if it was the slightly maniacal constancy of 'don't you *dare* touch my son' or just sheer admiration at the size of Dad's gumption, but the enormous man never threw a punch. He didn't even give a push. He took Dad on a long backwards walk down the field, eventually shrugging his hand off his collar, and then just walked away.

Dad paced over to me, put his arm around my shoulder, and asked if I was okay. I didn't know what to say. He seemed so powerful and unstoppable that I was a little bit starstruck. He had always been my hero, but in that moment, he was my *super*hero. He was better than Superman and Batman combined.

Once the dust settled on the 99, the last two minutes of the game were eventually played. I don't remember exactly what happened next, but I do remember that last kick to the sideline, followed by the long drawl of the final whistle. We had won.

I also remember the enormous man walking over and apologising to me and Dad for his behaviour. 'No worries, mate,' Dad replied. All was forgiven.

On the long drive home, I asked Dad all sorts of questions about what had happened. Even though I'd been right there, I begged him to tell me the story again and again. As he repeated it for the sixth time, I could tell he had a sense of pride for doing something that had meant so much to his son. I asked him if he'd been scared when the enormous man was staring down at him with his enormous head and his enormous eyes. He said that he hadn't really thought about it. He had just seen that I needed help, and the next part was simple.

The image of my dad – Keg – with his hand grabbing the enormous man's collar, walking backwards, is one of the strongest memories I have of him. In that moment, he demonstrated everything you need to know about his character. His unyielding love for his children and willingness to sacrifice anything to keep them safe. His determination to never be beaten by life, no matter the odds. And his brazen and slightly hazardous belief that the bigger they are, the harder they fall.

∞

I am sitting in the free 60-minute car park in front of Auckland's Mercy Hospital. Somewhere inside the rabbit warren of wards and waiting rooms, Dad is undergoing his third invasive heart operation in the last 15 years, another cardiac ablation. I am alone. Waiting for news on the outcome of a procedure – whether good or bad; I've had both – is agony.

I am not allowed in the waiting room this time because of COVID-19 restrictions. I re-park my car every hour so that I don't get a ticket. But I think the security guard who patrols the car park is catching on. Maybe I should park on the road. I just want to make sure that I'm close when the phone rings.

Dad is probably talking to the anaesthetist now. I imagine he is searching for a light-hearted connection, perhaps asking the doctor his name and then trying to find some common ground ('John Smith, eh – I don't suppose you're related to Jackie Smith from Kawakawa?'). Once Dad is alone, he will put on his headphones and play his favourite song on repeat: 'Comfortably Numb' by Pink Floyd. In the chorus, guitarist Dave Gilmour assumes the persona of a man remembering a fever he had as a boy, one that made his hands swell like two balloons – swell as Dad's heart did when he himself was a boy with a fever.

Sitting here, my mind is full of dark thoughts, flashes of terror. What if Dad dies on the operating table? If he does, will I see him again? Do I want to? And how will I tell Mum?

I try not to think about that. Now and then, a warm feeling washes over me, a reassuring sense that we have been here before and will pull through again. Maybe God or some higher power gives me strength. Maybe not. I don't know. But when those moments come, I hold on to them tightly, for as long as I can.

Acknowledgements

My dad, Keg, shared so much of himself and his story, and I will be forever grateful to him for allowing me to capture it. This book couldn't have happened without the love and support of Team Gurney – Sarah, Liv and Noah – or without my extremely clever mum, Chris, who always made me feel that I could do anything I set my mind to. Sarah – thank you for believing in me from the outset. To quote Thom Yorke: 'You are my centre when I spin away.'

My profound thanks to Professor Michael Baker for his comprehensive review of this book, including fact-checking and context-giving. Your collegiality and leadership made the RF RISK study happen. To Associate Professor Nikki Moreland for bringing her considerable immunological expertise to bear on early drafts – thank you for making me look smart. Sincere thanks to my mentor and dear friend, Professor Diana Sarfati, for reading an early draft and only saying nice things. To my clinical and Māori health mentor, Professor Jonathan Koea, for all the coffee and chin-wags, and my brother-in-music, Professor Chris Jackson, for pointing me in the direction of Atul Gawande.

To the excellent Otago University Press team, especially Sue Wootton and Fiona Moffat – thank you for believing in this project. Sincere thanks to Sue, Megan Kitching and Mel Stevens for caring as much about the final manuscript as I did. Also sincere thanks to Eric Trump for reviewing and editing early drafts. Ngā mihi nui to Heramaahina Eketone for the beautiful piece of art for the cover.

Rheumatic fever is a deeply unfair illness that should not exist in a high-income country. My final acknowledgement is to those who will be diagnosed tomorrow with a disease that could have been eradicated yesterday.

Notes

Chapter 1: Infection

1. T. Billroth, 'Historical studies on the nature and treatment of gunshot wounds from the fifteenth century to the present time', *Yale Journal of Biology and Medicine* 4(3), 1859, pp. 225–57.
2. T. Billroth, *Chirurgische Briefe aus den Kriegs-Lazarethen in Weissenburg und Mannheim 1870* (Berlin: A. Hirschwald, 1872).
3. T. Billroth, *Untersuchungen über die Vegetationsformen von Coccobacteria septica und den Antheil, welchen sie an der Entstehung und Verbreitung der accidentellen Wundkrankheiten haben: Versuch einer wissenschaftlichen Kritik der verschiedenen Methoden antiseptischer Wundbehandlung* (Berlin: G. Reimer, 1874).
4. T. Billroth, 'Coccobacteria Septica', *Edinburgh Medical Journal* 20(4), 1874, pp. 366–74.
5. H. Wang et al., 'Good or bad: Gut bacteria in human health and diseases', *Biotechnology and Biotechnological Equipment* 32(5), 2018, pp. 1075–80.
6. C. Zimmer, *A Planet of Viruses* (Chicago: University of Chicago Press, 2012).
7. H. Brüssow, 'Phages of Streptococcus Thermophilus', in *Encyclopedia of Virology*, eds A. Granoff and R.G. Webster (Oxford: Elsevier, 1999), pp. 1253–62; and M. Gobbetti and M. Calasso, 'Streptococcus: Introduction', in *Encyclopedia of Food Microbiology*, eds C.A. Batt and M.L. Tortorello (Oxford: Academic Press, 2014), pp. 535–53.
8. J. Andersen et al., 'Clinical features and epidemiology of septicaemia and meningitis in neonates due to Streptococcus agalactiae in Copenhagen county, Denmark: A 10-year survey from 1992 to 2001', *Acta Paediatrica, International Journal of Paediatrics* 93(10), 2004, pp. 1334–39.
9. D. Bogaert et al., 'Streptococcus pneumoniae colonisation: The key to pneumococcal disease', *Lancet Infectious Diseases* 4(3), 2004, pp. 144–54.
10. T.C. Smith, 'Streptococcus (Group A)', in *Deadly Diseases and Epidemics* (New York: Chelsea House Publishing, 2010).
11. T.J. Mitchell, 'The pathogenesis of streptococcal infections: From tooth decay to meningitis', *Nature Reviews Microbiology* 1(3), 2003, pp. 219–30.
12. G. Gherardi et al., 'Prevalent emm types among invasive GAS in Europe and North America since year 2000', *Frontiers in Public Health* 6, 2019, article 59; and A.C. Steer et al., 'Global emm type distribution of group A streptococci: systematic review and implications for vaccine development', *Lancet Infectious Diseases* 9(10), 2009, pp. 611–16.

13. N. Shaikh et al., 'Prevalence of streptococcal pharyngitis and streptococcal carriage in children: A meta-analysis', *Pediatrics 126*(3), 2010, pp. e557–64.
14. J. Steere-Williams, 'The germ theory', in *A Companion to the History of American Science*, eds G.M. Montgomery and M.A. Largent (New York: John Wiley & Sons, 2015), pp. 397–407.
15. C.C. Wang et al., 'Airborne transmission of respiratory viruses', *Science 373*(6558), 2021.
16. Smith, 'Streptococcus (Group A)'.
17. I. Semmelweis, *Etiology, Concept and Prophylaxis of Childbed Fever* (Madison and London: The University of Wisconsin Press, 1861).
18. K.C. Carter and B.R. Carter, *Childbed Fever. A scientific biography of Ignaz Semmelweis* (Oxford: Routledge, 2005).
19. A.C. Evans, 'Studies on Hemolytic Streptococci: II. Streptococcus pyogenes', *Journal of Bacteriology 31*(6), 1936, pp. 611–24.
20. A.R. Katz and D.M. Morens, 'Severe streptococcal infections in historical perspective', *Clinical Infectious Diseases 14*(1), 1992, pp. 298–307.
21. S. Brouwer et al., 'Pathogenesis, epidemiology and control of Group A Streptococcus infection', *Nature Reviews Microbiology 21*(7), 2023, pp. 431–47.
22. E. Klein, 'The etiology of scarlet fever', *Proceedings of the Royal Society of London 42*, 1887, pp. 158–61.
23. U. Katzenell et al., 'Streptococcal contamination of food: An unusual cause of epidemic pharyngitis', *Epidemiology and Infection 127*(2), 2001, pp. 179–84.
24. D.L. Stevens and A.E. Bryant, 'Streptococcus pyogenes Impetigo, Erysipelas, and Cellulitis', in *Streptococcus Pyogenes: Basic biology to clinical manifestations*, eds J.J. Ferretti et al. (Oklahoma City: University of Oklahoma Health Sciences Center, 2022).
25. B. Wilson, 'Necrotizing fasciitis', *The American Surgeon 18*(4), 1952, pp. 416–31.
26. M.J. Walker et al., 'Disease manifestations and pathogenic mechanisms of group A Streptococcus', *Clinical Microbiology Reviews 27*(2), 2014, pp. 264–301; and S. Schindehette, 'Legacy of a gentle genius', *People Magazine 33*(24), 1990, pp. 88–96.
27. S. Brooks, *Civil War Medicine* (Springfield: Charles C. Thomas, 1966), p. 84.
28. G.F. Dick and G.H. Dick, 'The etiology of scarlet fever', *Journal of the American Medical Association 82*(4), 1924, pp. 301–02.
29. R.H.C. Zegers et al., 'The death of Wolfgang Amadeus Mozart: An epidemiologic perspective', *Annals of Internal Medicine 151*(4), 2009, pp. 274–78.

Chapter 2: Response

1. M. Coates et al., 'Innate antimicrobial immunity in the skin: A protective barrier against bacteria, viruses, and fungi', *PLOS Pathogens 14*(12), 2018, e1007353.
2. E. Uribe-Querol and C. Rosales, 'Phagocytosis: Our current understanding of a universal biological process', *Frontiers in Immunology 11*, 2020, article 1066.

3. E. Kolaczkowska and P. Kubes, 'Neutrophil recruitment and function in health and inflammation', *Nature Reviews Immunology* 13(3), 2013, pp. 159–75.
4. H.N. Eisen and J.H. Pearce, 'The nature of antibodies and antigens', *Annual Review of Microbiology* 16(1), 1962, pp. 101–26.
5. S. Nagata and M. Tanaka, 'Programmed cell death and the immune system', *Nature Reviews Immunology* 17(5), 2017, pp. 333–40.
6. W. Ratajczak et al., 'Immunological memory cells', *Central European Journal of Immunology* 43(2), 2018, pp. 194–203.
7. T.J. Mitchell, 'The pathogenesis of streptococcal infections: From tooth decay to meningitis', *Nature Reviews Microbiology* 1(3), 2003, pp. 219–30.
8. N.J. Avire et al., 'A review of Streptococcus pyogenes: Public health risk factors, prevention and control', *Pathogens* 10(2), 2021, p. 248.
9. L.A. Kwinn and V. Nizet, 'How group A Streptococcus circumvents host phagocyte defenses', *Future Microbiology* 2(1), 2007, pp. 75–84.
10. S. Brouwer et al., 'Pathogenesis, epidemiology and control of Group A Streptococcus infection', *Nature Reviews Microbiology* 21(7), 2023, pp. 431–47.

Chapter 3: Rheumatic fever: Discovery, failure, repeat

1. P.C. English, 'Emergence of rheumatic fever in the nineteenth century', *The Milbank Quarterly* 67 (Suppl. 1), 1989, pp. 33–49.
2. F.W. Denny, 'A 45-year perspective on the streptococcus and rheumatic fever: The Edward H. Kass Lecture in infectious disease history', *Clinical Infectious Diseases* 19(6), 1994, pp. 1110–22; and L. Rantz, 'Hemolytic streptococcal infections', in *Preventive Medicine in World War II vol. 4* (Washington, DC: Office of the Surgeon General, 1958).
3. Denny, 'A 45-year perspective on the streptococcus and rheumatic fever', pp. 1110–22.
4. L. Gordis, 'The virtual disappearance of rheumatic fever in the United States: Lessons in the rise and fall of disease. T. Duckett Jones memorial lecture', *Circulation* 72(6), 1985, pp. 1155–62.
5. E.H. Kass, 'Infectious diseases and social change', *Journal of Infectious Diseases* 123(1), pp. 110–14.
6. R.C. Lancefield, 'The antigenic complex of Streptococcus Haemolyticus: I. Demonstration of a type-specific substance in extracts of Streptococcus Haemolyticus', *The Journal of Experimental Medicine* 47(1), 1928, pp. 91–103; and R.C. Lancefield, 'A serological differentiation of human and other groups of hemolytic streptococci', *The Journal of Experimental Medicine* 57(4), 1933, pp. 571–95.
7. S. Thomson and A.J. Glazebrook, 'Infectious diseases in a semiclosed community', *The Journal of Hygiene (London)* 41(5–6), 1941, pp. 570–615; C.A. Green, 'Serological examination of haemolytic Streptococci', *British Medical Journal* 1(4038), 1938, pp. 1147–49; J.F. Rinehart and S.R. Mettier, 'The heart valves and muscle in experimental scurvy with superimposed infection: With notes on the similarity of the

lesions to those of rheumatic fever', *American Journal of Pathology* 10(1), 1934, pp. 61–80; and S. Thomson and J. Innes, 'Haemolytic Streptococci in the cardiac lesions of acute rheumatism', *British Medical Journal* 2(4169), 1940, pp. 733–36.
8. L. Rantz, 'Hemolytic streptococcal infections' in *Preventive medicine in World War II. Vol 4: Communicable diseases transmitted chiefly through respiratory and alimentary tracts* (Washington, DC: Office of the Surgeon General, 1958).
9. Ibid.
10. D.S. Damrosch, 'Chemoprophylaxis and sulfonamide resistant streptococci', *Journal of the American Medical Association* 130(3), 1946, pp. 124–28.
11. Denny, 'A 45-year perspective on the streptococcus and rheumatic fever'.
12. E. Lax, *The Mold in Dr. Florey's Coat: The story of the penicillin miracle* (New York: Henry Holt and Company, LLC, 2005).
13. Rantz, 'Hemolytic streptococcal infections'.
14. Denny, 'A 45-year perspective on the streptococcus and rheumatic fever'; and Rantz, 'Hemolytic streptococcal infections'.
15. L. Rantz et al., 'Streptococcic and nonstreptococcic disease of the respiratory tract: Epidemiologic observations', *Archives of Internal Medicine* 77, 1946, pp. 121–31.
16. Rantz, 'Hemolytic streptococcal infections'.
17. W.B. Cheadle, 'Barbeian lectures on the various manifestations of the rheumatic state as exemplified in childhood and early life', *The Lancet* 133(3428), 1889, pp. 921–27; W.B. Cheadle, 'Barbeian lectures on the various manifestations of the rheumatic state as exemplified in childhood and early life', *The Lancet* 133(3427), 1889, pp. 871–77; and W.B. Cheadle, 'Barbeian lectures on the various manifestations of the rheumatic state as exemplified in childhood and early life', *The Lancet* 133(3426), 1889, pp. 821–27.
18. T.D. Jones, 'The diagnosis of rheumatic fever', *Journal of the American Medical Association* 126(8), 1944, pp. 481–84.
19. *New Zealand Guidelines for Rheumatic Fever: Diagnosis, management and secondary prevention of acute rheumatic fever and rheumatic heart disease* (Wellington, Heart Foundation of New Zealand, 2014 update).
20. T.J. Cone, *History of American Pediatrics* (Boston: Little Brown & Co., 1977).
21. Lax, *The Mold in Dr. Florey's Coat*.
22. Ibid.
23. A. Fleming, 'On the antibacterial action of cultures of a penicillium, with special reference to their use in the isolation of B. influenza', *British Journal of Experimental Pathology* 10(3), 1929, pp. 226–36.
24. Lax, *The Mold in Dr. Florey's Coat*.
25. C. Fletcher, 'First clinical use of penicillin', *British Medical Journal* 289(6460), 1984, pp. 1721–23; and Lax, *The Mold in Dr. Florey's Coat*.
26. Lax, *The Mold in Dr. Florey's Coat*.

Chapter 4: Gone, not gone

1. A.C. Steer and J.R. Carapetis, 'Prevention and treatment of rheumatic heart disease in the developing world', *Nature Reviews Cardiology* 6(11), 2009, pp. 689–98.

2. *New Zealand Guidelines for Rheumatic Fever: Diagnosis, management and secondary prevention of acute rheumatic fever and rheumatic heart disease* (Wellington: Heart Foundation of New Zealand, 2014 update).
3. F.W. Denny, 'A 45-year perspective on the streptococcus and rheumatic fever: The Edward H. Kass Lecture in infectious disease history', *Clinical Infectious Diseases 19*(6), 1994, pp. 1110–22.
4. T.J. Cone, *History of American Pediatrics* (Boston: Little Brown & Co., 1977).
5. Denny, 'A 45-year perspective on the streptococcus and rheumatic fever'.
6. L. Gordis, 'The virtual disappearance of rheumatic fever in the United States: Lessons in the rise and fall of disease. T. Duckett Jones memorial lecture', *Circulation 72*(6), 1985, pp. 1155–62.
7. E.H. Kass, 'Infectious diseases and social change', *Journal of Infectious Diseases 123*(1), 1971, pp. 110–14.
8. J. Spielvogel, 'The Industrial Revolution and its impact on European society', in *Western Civilization* (Boston: Cenage Learning, 2021).
9. B. Muhamed et al., 'Genetics of rheumatic fever and rheumatic heart disease', *Nature Reviews Cardiology 17*(3), 2020, pp. 145–54.
10. G. Karthikeyan and L. Guilherme, 'Acute rheumatic fever', *The Lancet 392*(10142), 2018, pp. 161–74.
11. Gordis, 'The virtual disappearance of rheumatic fever in the United States'.
12. Kass, 'Infectious diseases'.
13. J.R. Carapetis et al., 'Acute rheumatic fever and rheumatic heart disease', *Nature Reviews Disease Primers 2*(1), 2016, article 15084.
14. A. Coburn, 'Observations on the mechanism of rheumatic fever', *The Lancet 228*(5905), 1936, pp. 1025–30.
15. N. Lorenz et al., 'Serological profiling of group A Streptococcus infections in acute rheumatic fever', *Clinical Infectious Diseases 73*(12), 2021, pp. 2322–25.
16. G. de Crombrugghe et al., 'The limitations of the rheumatogenic concept for Group A Streptococcus: Systematic review and genetic analysis', *Clinical Infectious Diseases 70*(7), 2019, pp. 1453–60.
17. S.T. Shulman et al., 'Temporal changes in streptococcal M protein types and the near-disappearance of acute rheumatic fever in the United States', *Clinical Infectious Diseases 42*(4), 2006, pp. 441–47.
18. J.M. Stanhope, 'New Zealand trends in rheumatic fever: 1885–1971', *New Zealand Medical Journal 82*(551), 1975, pp. 297–99.
19. W.E. Morton and J.A. Lichty, 'Rheumatic heart disease epidemiology: II. Colorado's high-risk low-socioeconomic region in 1960', *American Journal of Epidemiology 92*(2), 1970, pp. 113–20.
20. No listed author, 'Community control of rheumatic heart disease in developing countries: a major public health problem', *WHO Chronicle 34*(9), 1980, pp. 336–45.
21. A. Arguedas and E. Mohs, 'Prevention of rheumatic fever in Costa Rica', *Journal of Pediatrics 121*(4), 1992, pp. 569–72.
22. S.S. Silva, 'Incidence of rheumatic fever in Ceylon', *Archives of Disease in Childhood 34*(175), 1959, pp. 247–49.

23. R. Negus, 'Rheumatic fever in Western Fiji: The female preponderance', *Medical Journal of Australia 2*, 1971, pp. 251–54.
24. J. Sievers and P. Hall, 'Incidence of acute rheumatic fever', *British Heart Journal* 33(6), 1971, pp. 833–36.
25. J.K. Gurney et al., 'The incidence of acute rheumatic fever in New Zealand, 2010–2013', *New Zealand Medical Journal* 128(1417), 2015, pp. 65–67.
26. J. Bennett et al., 'Rising ethnic inequalities in acute rheumatic fever and rheumatic heart disease, New Zealand, 2000–2018', *Emerging Infectious Diseases* 27(1), 2021, pp. 36–46.
27. *The Health and Welfare of Australia's Aboriginal and Torres Strait Islander Peoples* (Canberra, Australia: Australian Institute of Health ad Welfare, 2015).
28. Bennett et al., 'Rising ethnic inequalities in acute rheumatic fever and rheumatic heart disease', pp. 36–46.

Chapter 5: The long shadow

1. M.W. Cunningham, 'Molecular mimicry, autoimmunity, and infection: The cross-reactive antigens of group a Streptococci and their sequelae', *Microbiology Spectrum* 7(4), 2019.
2. J.R. Carapetis et al., 'Acute rheumatic fever and rheumatic heart disease', *Nature Reviews Disease Primers* 2(1), 2016, article 15084.
3. J.J. Noubiap et al., 'Prevalence and progression of rheumatic heart disease: a global systematic review and meta-analysis of population-based echocardiographic studies', *Scientific Reports* 9(1), 2019, article 17022.
4. E. Marijon et al., 'Rheumatic heart disease', *The Lancet* 379(9819), 2012, pp. 953–64.
5. B.J.J.M. Brundel et al., 'Atrial fibrillation', *Nature Reviews Disease Primers* 8(1), 2022, p. 21.
6. H. Souttar, 'The surgical treatment of mitral stenosis', *British Medical Journal* 2(3379), 1925, pp. 2603–06.
7. J. Dominik and P. Zacek, 'History of heart valve surgery', in *Heart Valve Surgery* (Berlin: Springer, 2010), pp. 13–19.
8. M. Russoa et al., 'The evolution of surgical valves', *Cardiovascular Medicine* 20(12), 2017, pp. 285–92.
9. D.N. Ross, 'Homograft replacement of the aortic valve', *The Lancet* 2(7254), 1962, p. 487; and R. Hopkins et al., 'Ross' first homograft replacement of the aortic valve', *Annals of Thoracic Surgery* 52(5), 1991, pp. 1190–93.
10. Dominik and Zacek, 'History of heart valve surgery'.
11. D.A. Watkins et al., 'Global, regional, and national burden of rheumatic heart disease, 1990–2015', *New England Journal of Medicine* 377(8), 2017, pp. 713–22.
12. A.C. Steer, 'Historical aspects of rheumatic fever', *Journal of Paediatrics and Child Health* 51(1), 2015, pp. 21–27.
13. J. Oliver et al., 'Progression of acute rheumatic fever to recurrence, rheumatic heart disease, and death in New Zealand children and youth: A cohort study', *Heart, Lung and Circulation* 28(S4), 2019.
14. D.A. Watkins et al., 'Global, regional, and national burden of rheumatic heart disease, 1990–2015', *New England Journal of Medicine* 377(8), 2017, pp. 713–22.

15. Ibid.
16. J. Bennett et al., 'Rising ethnic inequalities in acute rheumatic fever and rheumatic heart disease, New Zealand, 2000–2018', *Emerging Infectious Diseases* 27(1), 2021, pp. 36–46.
17. *The Health and Welfare of Australia's Aboriginal and Torres Strait Islander Peoples: 2015* (Canberra, Australia: Australian Institute of Health and Welfare, 2015).
18. Bennett et al., 'Rising ethnic inequalities in acute rheumatic fever and rheumatic heart disease'.

Chapter 6: The causes of rheumatic fever

1. *New Zealand Guidelines for Rheumatic Fever: Diagnosis, management and secondary prevention of acute rheumatic fever and rheumatic heart disease* (Wellington: Heart Foundation of New Zealand, 2014 update).
2. J.K. Gurney et al., 'Estimating the risk of acute rheumatic fever in New Zealand by age, ethnicity and deprivation', *Epidemiology and Infection* 144(14), 2016, pp. 3058–67.
3. Ibid.
4. S. Cartwright, 'The media and the murder house', *New Zealand Dental Journal* 106(1), 2010, pp. 7–12.
5. S.J. Jack et al., 'Primary prevention of rheumatic fever in the 21st century: Evaluation of a national programme', *International Journal of Epidemiology* 47(5), 2018, pp. 1585–93.
6. D. Lennon et al., 'School-based prevention of acute rheumatic fever: A group randomized trial in New Zealand', *Pediatric Infectious Disease Journal* 28(9), 2009, pp. 787–94.
7. S.J. Jack et al., 'Primary prevention of rheumatic fever in the 21st century: Evaluation of a national programme'.
8. A.C. Steer et al., 'Global emm type distribution of group A streptococci: systematic review and implications for vaccine development', *Lancet Infectious Diseases* 9(10), 2009, pp. 611–16.
9. G. de Crombrugghe et al.,'The limitations of the rheumatogenic concept for Group A Streptococcus: Systematic review and genetic analysis', *Clinical Infectious Diseases* 70(7), 2019, pp. 1453–60.
10. J.R. Carapetis et al., 'The global burden of group A streptococcal diseases', *Lancet Infectious Diseases* 5(11), 2005, pp. 685–94.
11. M. Sheel et al., 'Development of Group A streptococcal vaccines: an unmet global health need', *Expert Review of Vaccines* 15(2), 2016, pp. 227–38; 'The Australian Strep A Vaccine Initiative': www.asavi.org.au; and New Zealand Government (2021); 'Funding for vaccine development to help prevent rheumatic fever': www.beehive.govt.nz/release/funding-vaccine-development-help-prevent-rheumatic-fever
12. S. Riedel, 'Edward Jenner and the history of smallpox and vaccination', *Baylor University Medical Center Proceedings* 18(1), 2005, pp. 21–25.
13. J. Oliver et al., 'Preceding group A streptococcus skin and throat infections are individually associated with acute rheumatic fever: evidence from New Zealand', *BMJ Global Health* 6(12), 2021, article e007038.

14. Institute of Environmental Science and Research, 'Rheumatic Fever Reports 2014–2018': www.surv.esr.cri.nz/surveillance/RheumaticFever
15. A.F. Coburn, 'Observations on the mechanism of rheumatic fever', *The Lancet* 228(5905), 1936, pp. 1025–30.
16. T. Turia, *All About Equity: Building political will for rheumatic fever prevention in New Zealand* (Melbourne: World Congress of Cardiology, 2014).
17. H. Vlajinac et al., 'Influence of socio-economic and other factors on rheumatic fever occurrence', *European Journal of Epidemiology* 7(6), 1991, pp. 702–04.
18. F. Li et al., 'Obesity and the built environment: Does the density of neighborhood fast-food outlets matter?', *American Journal of Health Promotion* 23(3), 2009, pp. 203–09; and C.A. Campbell et al., 'The effectiveness of limiting alcohol outlet density as a means of reducing excessive alcohol consumption and alcohol-related harms', *American Journal of Preventive Medicine* 37(6), 2009, pp. 556–69.
19. M.G. Baker et al., 'Risk factors for acute rheumatic fever: A case-control study', *The Lancet* 26(100508), 2022.
20. M.G. Baker et al., 'Risk factors'; P.E. Grave, 'Social and environmental factors in the aetiology of rheumatic fever', *Medical Journal of Australia* 44(18), 1957, pp. 602–08; B. Adanja et al., 'Socioeconomic factors in the etiology of rheumatic fever', *Journal of Hygiene, Epidemiology, Microbiology and Immunology* 32(3), 1988, pp. 329–35; D.K. Kurahara et al., 'Ethnic differences for developing rheumatic fever in a low-income group living in Hawaii', *Ethnicity and Disease* 16(2), 2006, pp. 357–61; and B.K. Riaz et al., 'Risk factors of rheumatic heart disease in Bangladesh: A case-control study', *Journal of Health, Population and Nutrition* 31(1), 2013, pp. 70–77.
21. P. Howden-Chapman and N. Pierse, 'Commentary on housing, health, and well-being in Aotearoa/New Zealand', *Health Education and Behavior* 47(6), 2020, pp. 802–04.
22. J. Oliver et al., 'Preceding group A streptococcus skin and throat infections are individually associated with acute rheumatic fever: Evidence from New Zealand', *BMJ Global Health* 6(12), 2021; M.G. Baker et al., 'Risk factors'; and S. Thomas et al., 'Descriptive analysis of group A Streptococcus in skin swabs and acute rheumatic fever, Auckland, New Zealand, 2010–2016', *Lancet Regional Health Western Pacific* 8(100101), 2021.
23. J. Bennett et al., 'Risk factors for group A streptococcal pharyngitis and skin infections: A case control study', *Lancet Regional Health Western Pacific* 26(100507), 2022, pp. 1–9.

Chapter 7: The causes of the causes—Part I

1. M. Carter et al., *Healthy Homes Initiative Evaluation* (Wellington: Allen and Clarke, 2018).
2. M. Sims et al., 'Importance of housing and cardiovascular health and well-being: A scientific statement from the American Heart Association', *Circulation: Cardiovascular Quality and Outcomes* 13(8), 2020, e000089;

J.R. Oliver et al., 'Acute rheumatic fever and exposure to poor housing conditions in New Zealand: A descriptive study', *Journal of Paediatrics and Child Health* 53(4), 2017, pp. 358–64.
3. J. Oliver et al., 'Risk of rehospitalisation and death for vulnerable New Zealand children', *Archives of Disease in Childhood* 103(4), 2018, pp. 327–34.
4. P. Howden-Chapman and N. Pierse, 'Commentary on housing, health, and well-being in Aotearoa/New Zealand', *Health Education and Behavior* 47(6), 2020, pp. 802–04.
5. *Indoor environment: Health aspects of air quality, thermal environment, light and noise* (Geneva, Switzerland: World Health Organisation, 1990).
6. 'OECD Environmental Performance Reviews: New Zealand, 2017': www.oecd.org; and *WHO Housing and health guidelines* (Geneva, Switzerland: World Health Organisation, 2018).
7. T. Ingham et al., 'Damp mouldy housing and early childhood hospital admissions for acute respiratory infection: A case control study', *Thorax* 74(9), 2019, pp. 849–57.
8. P. Howden-Chapman et al., 'The effects of housing on health and well-being in Aotearoa New Zealand', *New Zealand Population Review 47*, 2021, pp. 16–32.
9. M.G. Baker et al., 'Risk factors for acute rheumatic fever: A case-control study', *The Lancet* 26(100508), 2022.
10. A. Johnson et al., *A Stocktake of New Zealand's Housing* (Wellington: New Zealand Centre for Sustainable Cities, 2018).
11. Ibid.
12. N. Pierse et al., 'Well Homes Initiative: A home-based intervention to address housing-related ill health', *Health Education and Behavior* 47(6), 2020, pp. 836–44.
13. *Programme Review: Warm Up New Zealand* (Wellington: Ministry of Business, Innovation and Employment, 2017).
14. Energy Efficiency and Conservation Authority, 2018. 'Warmer Kiwi Homes Programme': www.eeca.govt.nz/co-funding/insulation-and-heater-grants/warmer-kiwi-homes-programme
15. C. Fyfe et al., 'Association between home insulation and hospital admission rates: Retrospective cohort study using linked data from a national intervention programme', *British Medical Journal 371*, 2020, article m4571.
16. M. Carter et al., *Healthy Homes Initiative Evaluation* (Wellington: Allen and Clarke, 2018).
17. N. Pierse et al., *Healthy Homes Initiative Outcomes Evaluation Service: Initial analysis of health outcomes* (Wellington: University of Otago, 2019).
18. New Zealand Government, 'Resource Management (Enabling Housing Supply and Other Matters) Amendment Act 2021': www.legislation.govt.nz/act/public/2021/0059/latest/LMS566049.html
19. Ministry of Pacific Island Affairs, *Demographics of New Zealand's Pacific population* (Wellington: Statistics New Zealand, 2010); and *Future Demographic Trends for Māori – Part Two* (Wellington: Te Puni Kōkiri, 2018).
20. Ministry of Housing and Urban Development, 2023, 'Public housing plan': www.hud.govt.nz/our-work/public-housing-plan

21. N. Pierse et al., 'Service usage by a New Zealand Housing First cohort prior to being housed', *SSM Population Health 8*, 2019, article 100432.
22. He Kāinga Oranga – Housing and Health, 2014, 'The rental housing warrant of fitness': www.healthyhousing.org.nz/our-research/past-research/rental-housing-warrant-fitness
23. L. Telfar-Barnard et al., 'Measuring the effect of housing quality interventions: The case of the New Zealand "Rental Warrant of Fitness"', *International Journal of Environmental Research and Public Health 14*(11), 2017, p. 1352.
24. He Kāinga Ora Housing and Health, 2023, 'First home loan': www.kaingaora.govt.nz/home-ownership/first-home-loan
25. Y. Yang and M. Rehm, 'Housing prices and speculation dynamics: A study of Auckland housing market', *Journal of Property Research 38*(4), 2021, pp. 286–304.
26. 'Quotable Value (QV) House Price Index 2024': www.qv.co.nz/price-index/
27. Johnson et al., *A Stocktake of New Zealand's Housing*.
28. *Programme Review: Warm Up New Zealand* (Wellington: Ministry of Business, Innovation and Employment, 2017).
29. 'Statistics New Zealand. Child poverty statistics: Year ended June 2023': www.stats.govt.nz/information-releases/child-poverty-statistics-year-ended-june-2023/

Chapter 8: The causes of the causes—Part II

1. HealthPoint, Auckland City Hospital: www.healthpoint.co.nz/auckland-city-hospital/
2. HealthPoint, Te Whare Oranga 2024: www.healthpoint.co.nz/gps-accident-urgent-medical-care/nurse-led-practice/te-whare-oranga/
3. M. Harwood et al., 'An audit of a marae-based health centre management of COVID-19 community cases in South Auckland', *New Zealand Medical Journal 135*(1549), 2022, pp. 120–28
4. Papakura Marae, 'Our Services 2024': www.papakuramarae.co.nz/services
5. National Hauora Coalition, 'Mana Kidz 2024': www.nhc.maori.nz/matou-mahi/our-programmes/mana-kidz; A. Anderson et al., 'Pacific Fono: A community-based initiative to improve rheumatic fever service delivery for Pacific Peoples in South Auckland', *Journal of Primary Health Care 12*(4), 2020, pp. 384–90; and P. Anderson et al., 'Nurse-led school-based clinics for rheumatic fever prevention and skin infection management: Evaluation of Mana Kidz programme in Counties Manukau', *The New Zealand Medical Journal 129*(1428), 2016, pp. 37–46.
6. J. Key, 'Maiden Speech: John Key MP for Helensville', 2002.
7. P. Crampton, 'Oh my', *New Zealand Medical Journal 133*(1524), 2020, pp. 8–10.
8. Statistics New Zealand, '2023 Census population counts (by ethnic group, age, and Māori descent) and dwelling counts': www.stats.govt.nz/information-releases/2023-census-population-counts-by-ethnic-group-age-and-maori-descent-and-dwelling-counts/
9. H. Leahy, *Crossing the floor: The story of Tariana Turia* (Wellington: Huia, 2015); and L. Humpage, 'Does

having an indigenous political party in government make a difference to social policy? The Māori Party in New Zealand', *Journal of Social Policy* 46(3), 2017, pp. 475–94.
10. S.J. Jack et al., 'Primary prevention of rheumatic fever in the 21st century: Evaluation of a national programme', *International Journal of Epidemiology* 47(5), 2018, pp. 1585–93; and D. Lennon et al., 'First presentation acute rheumatic fever is preventable in a community setting: A school-based intervention', *Pediatric Infectious Disease Journal* 36(12), 2017, pp. 1113–18.
11. S.J. Jack, D. Williamson, Y. Galloway et al., *Interim Evaluation of the Sore Throat Component of the Rheumatic Fever Prevention Programme – Quantitative Findings* (Porirua: The Institute of Environmental Science and Research Ltd., 2015).
12. *Rheumatic fever report 2022/2023* (Wellington: Te Whatu Ora, 2023).
13. 'Pū Manawa – Rheumatic Fever Network Aotearoa New Zealand': www.pumanawa.org.nz
14. Te Whatu Ora, 'Rheumatic Fever Roadmap, 2023–2028': www.tewhatuora.govt.nz/publications/rheumatic-fever-roadmap-2023-2028/
15. New Zealand Government, 'Child Poverty Reduction Act 2018': www.legislation.govt.nz/act/public/2018/0057/latest/LMS8294.html
16. M. Duncanson et al., *Child Poverty Monitor 2020 Technical Report* (Dunedin: Child and Youth Epidemiology Service, University of Otago, 2020).
17. J. Oliver et al., 'Preceding group A streptococcus skin and throat infections are individually associated with acute rheumatic fever: Evidence from New Zealand', *BMJ Global Health* 6(12), 2021, e007038; and M.G. Baker et al., 'Risk factors for acute rheumatic fever: A case-control study', *The Lancet* 26(100508), 2022.
18. J. Cooper et al., '"Hurts less, lasts longer": A qualitative study on experiences of young people receiving high-dose subcutaneous injections of benzathine penicillin G to prevent rheumatic heart disease in New Zealand', *PLoS One* 19(5), 2024, article e0302493.

Chapter 9: The path forward

1. M. Harwood et al., 'An audit of a marae-based health centre management of COVID-19 community cases in South Auckland', *New Zealand Medical Journal* 135(1549), 2022, pp. 120–28.
2. *Health and Disability System Review – Final Report – Pūrongo Whakamutunga* (Wellington: Health and Disability System Review, 2020).
3. *The New Zealand Medical Workforce in 2021* (Wellington: Medical Council of New Zealand, 2022).
4. J. Bennett et al., 'Rising ethnic inequalities in acute rheumatic fever and rheumatic heart disease, New Zealand, 2000–2018', *Emerging Infectious Diseases* 27(1), 2021, pp. 36–46.
5. Statistics New Zealand, 'National and subnational period life tables: 2017–2019': www.stats.govt.nz/information-releases/national-and-subnational-period-life-tables-2017-2019

6. *He Pūrongo Mate Pukupuku o Aotearoa 2020 – The State of Cancer in New Zealand 2020* (Wellington: Te Aho o Te Kahu – Cancer Control Agency, 2021).
7. L.G. Gordon et al., 'Estimated healthcare costs of melanoma and keratinocyte skin cancers in Australia and Aotearoa New Zealand in 2021', *International Journal of Environmental Research and Public Health 19*(6), 2022, p. 3178.
8. B. Obama, *The Audacity of Hope* (New York: Crown / Three Rivers Press, 2006).
9. Heart Foundation of New Zealand, 'New Zealand Guidelines for Rheumatic Fever: Diagnosis, management and secondary prevention of acute rheumatic fever and rheumatic heart disease: 2019 update': www.heartfoundation.org.nz/resources/acute-rheumatic-fever-and-rheumatic-heart-disease-guideline
10. J. Cooper et al., '"Hurts less, lasts longer": A qualitative study on experiences of young people receiving high-dose subcutaneous injections of benzathine penicillin G to prevent rheumatic heart disease in New Zealand', *PLoS One 19*(5), 2024, article e0302493.
11. R.K. Barr et al., 'Development of a sustained release implant of benzathine penicillin G for secondary prophylaxis of rheumatic heart disease', *European Journal of Pharmaceutics and Biopharmaceutics 189*, 2023, pp. 240–50.

KA HAEA TE ATA

'Ka haea te ata' is the first line from a Kāi Tahu karakia that welcomes the dawn.

Ka Haea Te Ata books cast light on a variety of contemporary issues as the authors contemplate how we live – and how we could live – in Aotearoa New Zealand.

Other titles in this series:

Notes on Womanhood: A conversation about gender and identity
by Sarah Jane Barnett

Heart Stood Still: A conversation about belonging
by Miriam Sharland

Published by Otago University Press
Te Whare Tā o Ōtākou Whakaihu Waka
533 Castle Street
Dunedin, New Zealand
university.press@otago.ac.nz
www.oup.nz/press

First published 2024
Text copyright © Jason Gurney

The moral rights of the author have been asserted.

ISBN 978-1-99004879-1

A catalogue record for this book is available from the National Library of New Zealand. This book is copyright. Except for the purpose of fair review, no part may be stored or transmitted in any form or by any means, electronic or mechanical, including recording or storage in any information retrieval system, without permission in writing from the publishers. No reproduction may be made, whether by photocopying or by any other means, unless a licence has been obtained from the publisher.

Design: Fiona Moffat
Typesetting: Mel Stevens
Cover artwork: Heramaahina Eketone

Printed in Aotearoa New Zealand by Ligare.